Introduction to Real-time Software Design

Introduction to
Real-time Software Design

S. T. Allworth

Springer-Verlag New York Inc.

First published 1981 in the United Kingdom by
The Macmillan Press Ltd
Sole distributors in the USA:
Springer-Verlag New York Inc.
175 Fifth Avenue
New York, NY 10010
USA

ISBN-13: 978-1-4612-9085-8   e-ISBN-13: 978-1-4612-4610-7
DOI: 10.1007/978-1-4612-4610-7

to Leyla

Contents

Preface

In 1977 I was asked to prepare a series of twenty lectures introducing the design of real-time software to undergraduate electrical engineers at the University of Essex. At that time the advent of low-cost microprocessors was causing a minor revolution in the computer industry. The decreasing cost of hardware resulted in a mushrooming of the number of real-time applications being attempted. Many of these innovations were conducted by electrical engineers with little software background, or by computer scientists familiar only with large software systems. Even now future engineers still in training will have only a limited exposure to software because of the pressure of other subjects in their curricula. It was clear that a concise set of lectures, directed at people with limited exposure to software design was needed.

In order to find a suitable text I turned to the existing computer science literature. I discovered that the available material was scattered over a large number of reports and articles and varied widely in level of complexity. Nowhere was the information collected in a form useful to the beginner. It has been shown that by using a carefully structured approach to the subject, the mysteries of compiler writing, operating systems and databases can be made comprehensible, indeed straightforward, for the uninitiated. However, the subject of real-time software appeared still to be relegated to the realm of the black arts. In an attempt to bring this subject into the light I have extended my original series of notes into book form.

It is my belief that by applying a strong structural discipline to the design of real-time software it can be made a relatively straightforward task. Indeed, the increasing cost and diversity of real-time software will make simplification of the design task an imperative.

Chapter 1 introduces the topic in general, and puts forward the virtual machine concept as a fundamental design tool. Part I looks at how such a machine can be constructed: chapter 2 describes the machine, and chapters 3, 4 and 5 discuss the nucleus of the machine, scheduling and reliability considerations. Part II discusses the design of the processes that make up a real-time system: chapter 6 discusses general design philosophy, and chapter 7 introduces a number of useful process virtual machines. Part III discusses techniques for measuring and predicting system performance.

This book is intended to be a concise introduction to the subject of real-time software. It does not claim to offer total coverage of the topic. I do not attempt to describe areas that are currently the basis for research, or to detail existing systems; rather, I hope to outline general principles.

The design of real-time software has traditionally been the realm of the élite few involved in the construction of large operating and on-line systems. Increasingly, however, the computer scientist and engineer is finding that his job involves not only applications programming but the design of real-time software for mini and microprocessor systems. I hope that the following chapters will provide a clear introductory framework of the techniques used in this area of software design.

ACKNOWLEDGEMENTS

I should like to thank a number of people who have assisted me in writing this book. First and foremost I must thank Frank Coakley, my colleague on many real-time software courses. His advice, knowledge and criticism have contributed greatly to the book in its current form. Thanks also to Kevin Cox, Mick Langfield and Ian Witten, for their patience and helpful comments, and to the University of Essex, Cable and Wireless Ltd, and the Canberra College of Advanced Education, for their generous assistance.

Particular thanks to friends and family: to Jane, for diligently typing and weathering the storms, and to Margot Tolmer and the Irvings of Mill Farm, for providing kind understanding, shelter and support.

STEVE ALLWORTH

1 Introduction

Over the past few years the dramatic decrease in the cost of computing hardware has led to a proliferation of real-time systems in a wide range of applications. Most of the systems now being introduced are used to control commercial, industrial and communications systems. Even domestic devices and automobiles are incorporating real-time systems. The facilities required of the software in these applications vary as widely as the style of application. As a result it has become necessary to develop a set of generalised real-time software design techniques that are useful in the full range of applications. However, before this can be attempted it is necessary to define the properties that such systems have in common.

1.1 WHAT ARE REAL-TIME SYSTEMS?

Many attempts have been made to define a 'real-time' system. At best these definitions are incomplete and do not encompass all the characteristics of such a system. Rather than attempt an accurate definition, we shall discuss the properties and facilities that are commonly regarded as making up a real-time system.

1.1.1 Control Systems

A real-time system reacts so as to affect the environment in which it is operating. It is a collection of devices, controlled by a stored program of instructions. This program acts as the regulating element in a feedback loop, which then forms part of a commercial or industrial system.

For convenience, we shall divide the entire real-time system into two parts — the *controlled system* and the *controlling system*. The controlled system consists of the hardware devices which go to make up the part of the system that interfaces with the environment. The controlling system consists of the software element together with its associated processing hardware.

The configuration and behaviour of the components that constitute the controlled system vary with the purpose of the system. In a data-processing environment the devices may be terminals, disc drives, line printers and card

readers; they may be multiplexers, line drivers and teleprinters in a telecommunications environment; or indeed, they may be valves, relays or hoppers
in a process-control environment. Normally, the various devices do not function
completely independently of one another. In an air-conditioning system, for
instance, the heating element will usually have some knowledge of the action
of the fan, so that an even temperature of ducted air can be maintained.

A definition of a real-time system, then, must include the fact that it is
a control system. The design of the controlled system is very much system
dependent. However, the design of the controlling software can, hopefully, be
generalised. This book will attempt to define a set of design techniques and
guidelines that will be of use in producing such software.

1.1.2 Software Systems

Perhaps, if we analyse a range of software systems, we will be able to derive a
closer definition of the software controlling a real-time system.

Batch Accounting Systems

Most computers are used in the control of accounting and administrative systems.
The computer system does not normally control the business system directly.
Rather, it processes the data which are used for administrative control. A
commercial computing system is a collection of applications programs: data
verification, payroll, database management and other financial calculations.
These programs manipulate data and thus assist indirectly in the control of
the business system. In a conventional 'batch' system, these programs are run
in batches, selected in such a way as to optimise the use of computing facilities.
Because the computer system does not exercise immediate control over the
business system, and therefore the programs do not have to be run with stringent
time constraints, we will not consider this collection of batch applications
programs as being a real-time system.

On-line Systems

Most modern business computer systems are based on fully on-line operation.
An on-line system acts so as to maintain continuous control of a business
system. It does this by ensuring that, as each transaction occurs, the relevant
files and reports are updated before the next transaction affecting these files
is handled. This implies that the applications programs are not always run at
times dictated by the optimum use of computing resources. Instead they are
run at times imposed by requests from an environment of enquiry terminals,
point-of-sale terminals and other devices that are designed to input individual
queries or transactions.

The software controlling an on-line system is therefore extremely time critical. It is this *time-critical* aspect that differentiates an on-line system from a batch system, and qualifies it as a real-time system. The large number of on-line systems currently in operation constitutes the bulk of all real-time systems.

Operating Systems

Most modern computer installations have a collection of programs which control the computing system itself. These programs, making up the operating system, are designed to (1) control the devices that make up the hardware of the system, (2) ensure that the hardware resources of the system are employed optimally; and (3) provide utility programs such as editors and file-organisation facilities. The device-control programs, interrupt handling routines and other software at the nucleus of a multiprocessing operating system can be regarded as a real-time system. The controlled system in this case consists of the disc drives, printers and similar devices that make up the computer system itself.

Process-control and Communications Systems

Process-control systems include those for controlling chemical plants, missile systems, manufacturing machinery and, nowadays, individual automobiles. Communication systems include computer-controlled telephone exchanges and computer networks. The fact that a real-time system is working as a controlling element in a *time-critical* environment becomes very evident when viewing these applications. Another aspect that emerges when considering this area of application is that the software must be *reliable*. Large sums of money, valuable equipment and often human lives depend on the correct and reliable operation of the software controlling these systems.

1.1.3 General Properties

From the discussion to date, we can see that real-time software must be that which works in a time-critical environment to control some system of devices. However, since real-time systems are usually created to be part of marketable products, it is necessary to extend our description still further.

Responsiveness

In order to control its environment successfully, a real-time system must be *responsive* to changes in its environment. It is this responsiveness that forms the fundamental property of a real-time system. Unless the system reacts sufficiently rapidly, it cannot be considered to be operating in real-time. This property is usually quantified as the system's *response time.* The response time of a system is the time that the system will take to react to a change in, or stimulus from, its environment. The response time must be such that the system appears to react 'instantaneously'. What is regarded as an 'instantaneous' reaction will vary with the device. For a power-station boiler, 'instantaneous' may mean reaction to a temperature change within thirty minutes. For the system controlling a missile, the reaction to a course change must occur within a few milliseconds.

Correctness and Completeness

A real-time system should accurately and totally control an aspect of the environment. To be effective, then, the system must be *correct* and *complete.* It must be complete in the sense that it has catered for all possible eventualities and situations that may arise in the environment or in the controlling software itself. It must be correct, in that suitable decisions are made when the different situations arise (even if the decision is to do nothing at all). A wide range of situations and conditions occur in a real-world environment, and so it is extremely difficult completely and correctly to specify the requirements of a system designed to influence or control a portion of the real world. Before a real-time system can be designed, a requirement specification must be produced. Ideally the requirement specification must rigorously describe the action to be taken for every situation that the system will face. This is often the most difficult aspect of the project, and much of the final correctness of the system will depend on its success.

Reliability

A real-time system must be *reliable.* It must be able to provide a service that can be closely defined in terms of guaranteed minimum mean time between failure and mean time to repair. The system must 'fail softly' — it must provide a useful degraded service in the face of hardware failure. An example of the stringent reliability requirements imposed upon real-time systems is a stored-program-controlled telephone exchange. It may be expected to operate over a forty-year period with no more than a total of two hours out of service, depending on the degree of degradation of service.

Economy

The *cost* of instantaneous response, completeness, total correctness and absolute reliability must be taken into account when considering these ideals. As with any product, the designer will be constrained in his pursuit of an ideal design by economic considerations. An on-line system that guarantees a maximum response time of half a second may not be able to compete with a system that only offers a response time of two seconds, but sells at half the price!

In order to maintain its commercial viability, a real-time system must be as inexpensive to produce, run and maintain as possible. The following section will discuss this aspect in more detail.

1.2 SOFTWARE COSTS

The continuing reduction in the cost of computer hardware has not been parallelled by a corresponding drop in the cost of software. When attempting to analyse the factors behind this situation it is important to remember that real-time software is a *commercial product.* The form of the design of any product will influence the cost of manufacture, and the cost of maintaining the product over its lifetime. One purpose of this book is to discuss techniques that can be applied when designing real-time software, such that the over-all cost of the product is reduced. As a first step, we shall attempt to define the causes of high cost in software. This will point the way toward techniques which produce more economical designs.

1.2.1 Life-cycle Costs

When calculating the cost of any product it is necessary to analyse the costs throughout the *entire* life cycle of the product — not just the initial cost of production.

Hardware

Tracing the life cycle of a hardware product is reasonably elementary. A need (or market) is established, and the product is designed and manufactured. After being commissioned, the product enters a maintenance phase where worn parts are replaced and the product is serviced to ensure reliable operation. At a certain point in the product's life, the maintenance costs start to increase.

This occurs as the product nears the end of its useful life. At a certain point it is scrapped. The cost of the product versus time, over its lifetime, is shown in figure 1.1

Software

The software element of a real-time system has similar phases in its life cycle,

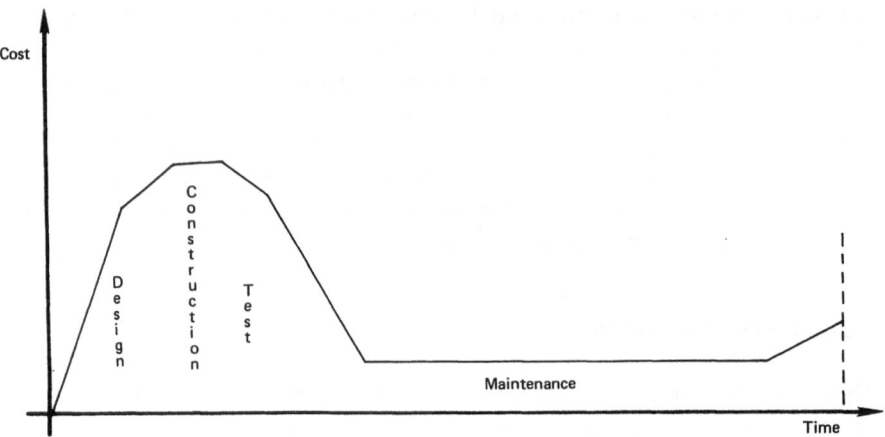

Figure 1.1 Hardware life cycle costs

but note, from figure 1.2, that the curve displays a radically different picture. The maintenance phase is a much greater factor in the product's lifetime cost. Software is far easier to change than hardware; it can be readily adapted to suit changing conditions and requirements. It is for this reason that the maintenance aspect will always dominate software costs.

Conventionally, maintaining a system means replacing parts that no longer carry out their function. By its very nature, software cannot 'wear out', but it can malfunction, or the functions required of it can change as time goes by. Maintenance in software terms means *changing* the software to repair shortcomings or modify its behaviour. Only in software that is not changed and is totally stable throughout its lifetime will the curve in figure 1.2 follow that of a hardware product.

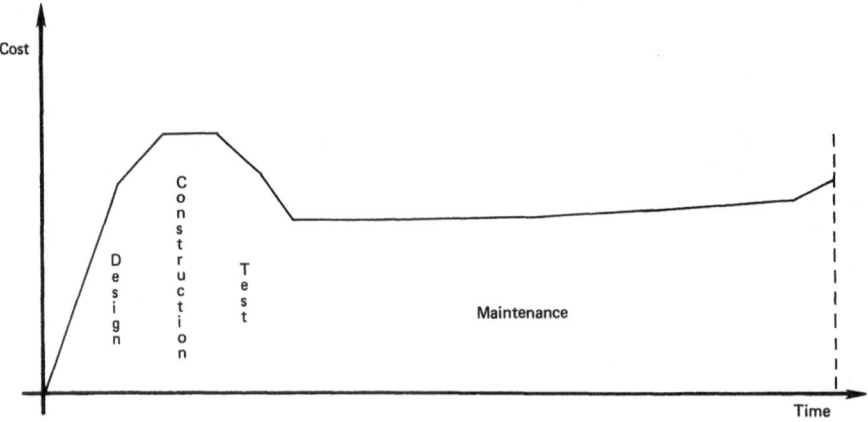

Figure 1.2 Software life cycle costs

So, if we can reduce the cost of maintenance, we' should be able to reduce the over-all cost of the product. Now, what causes high maintenance costs? As a result of studying the behaviour of a number of large software systems over their life cycle, Belady and Lehman (1974) proposed six 'laws', two of which are the following

> *The law of continuing change:* a system that is used undergoes continuing change until it is judged more cost effective to freeze and recreate it.
> *The law of increasing unstructuredness:* the entropy (disorder) of a system increases with time unless specific work is executed to maintain or reduce it.

In other words the product becomes more and more disordered as time goes by. This is reflected in the gradually rising cost curve shown in figure 1.2. It eventually becomes so complex that it becomes unacceptably difficult to maintain. It is the complexity inherent in the product that results in the high cost of maintenance and, at the beginning of the life cycle, in the high cost of production.

Complexity

A major contributing factor to the high cost of software is its complexity. Consider for a moment a mechanical analogy. Mechanical contrivances vary in complexity. If the contrivance is a simple device with one or two moving parts, then its production and maintenance are reasonably straightforward tasks. However, as the device becomes more intricate, with a great number of moving parts, production and maintenance become more difficult. If all the moving parts are interconnected in different ways, then the situation becomes even more complicated.

The creators of mechanical systems attempt to alleviate these problems by developing highly modular designs. The device is designed as a number of subassemblies, each subassembly being broken down into smaller units. The designer attempts to make each of these subassemblies as independent as possible, so that the installation of a new part requires as little work and causes as little disruption as possible. Modern technology abounds with plug-in pull-out disposable, sealed subassemblies — for sound economic reasons!

Turning once again to the software environment, it requires a surprisingly small amount of program code before a piece of software becomes incomprehensible to the human mind. A mechanical engineer would blanch at the prospect of constructing a contrivance consisting of one hundred thousand individual pieces. However, a software system of one hundred thousand instructions is considered medium sized. The potential complexity inherent in even a small software system is immense. If it is to be constructed economically, and economically maintained, then complexity must be minimised.

Structure

The way to reduce this complexity is to impose a strong modular structure on software design. Unless a structure is imposed at the design and construction stage, it may well prove impossible to manage the building of the system in the first place. If software is not constructed in a highly structured manner, then its complexity will result in errors difficult to detect during the testing phase. These errors will appear gradually as time goes by and will demand constant maintenance. In non-structured software, the very act of correcting one error may propagate other errors — a function of the intricate interconnection of all the system's parts.

In order to lower maintenance costs a software system may be 'frozen', but this is not always a solution. Inevitably inaccuracies and shortcomings are discovered in the requirement specification and changes must be made. The stringent reliability requirements imposed upon real-time systems imply that the software should contain minimum errors when delivered, and that any enhancements to the system should introduce a minimum of new errors. Strongly structured software has been shown to be the most powerful means of reducing such errors.

In the ensuing chapters we will see that it is possible to enforce the necessary structure on real-time software, from the over-all design right down to the individual lines of program code.

1.3   VIRTUAL MACHINES

The design of real-time software appears, at first sight, to be an extremely difficult task. On the one hand, we have a complex and often hazily defined problem area and, on the other, a hardware processor that is only capable of carrying out simple instructions. The designer must create a design for a large program of simple instructions which will satisfy the requirements of an ill-defined problem area. Fortunately, tools and techniques are available to assist this mapping of problem to machine.

1.3.1 Defining the Problem

Before the construction of a software system can commence, the designer must be completely clear as to what is required of the system. Formalised requirement specification and documentation techniques have been developed to assist in defining the problem. Examples include structured analysis and design technique (SADT) (Ross, 1977) and specification and design language (SDL) (CCITT, 1976). All such techniques are aimed at producing a highly structured document which precisely and completely defines the system to be built. They are often in graphical form and include a rigid set of rules aimed at highlighting areas where the specification is vague or incomplete.

1.3.2 Implementing the Solution

Designers represent their designs as symbolic models. An architect uses a scaled drawing to describe what will eventually be a three-dimensional structure. Electrical engineers use circuit diagrams to represent what will be a complex of electrical components. Physicists use mathematical formulae.

Software designs are expressed as data structures which model items in the problem area, and the actions which will manipulate this data. When implemented, the design will result in a program made up of the simple instructions and data items necessary for currently available computer hardware.

If there were available a machine that could use, as its basic software, the requirement specification document, then the software design problem would be solved. It would be necessary to describe accurately the system to be built and then this description would serve as the software model.

Unfortunately, such a machine does not exist as physical hardware. Currently available computer hardware cannot use, as its basic software, the forms of symbolic model that would best represent the application areas. We can, however, create such a machine. This machine, a *virtual machine*, is created by placing layers of software between the user and the hardware. The layers of software create successive virtual machines or *levels of abstraction*, each successive layer forming a more sophisticated machine whose attributes are more closely tailored to the designer's requirements. The software comprising each virtual machine layer automatically translates the data and actions which define the machine at that layer into the simpler data structures and actions which define the previous layer.

This automatic translation of higher-level abstractions into detailed lower-level operations achieves a significant reduction in over-all system complexity. If no virtual machine exists, then the designer must be aware of the detailed operation of the physical hardware. In this case the final design specification will be extremely complex, since it must closely specify a physical machine level program. In many ways the designer will be creating a solution to hardware idiosyncracies, rather than a solution to the problem at hand.

Consider figure 1.3. From the direction of the problem, or system to be designed, formalised specification and design techniques provide the designer with a more structured and well-defined description of the problem.

From the direction of the hardware, successive layers of software provide the designer with a more and more convenient virtual machine.

It remains to the designer to create a mapping between the requirement specification and the data and actions required for the virtual machine. This job is not easy. However, it is certainly less complex than trying to map the problem directly onto the physical hardware.

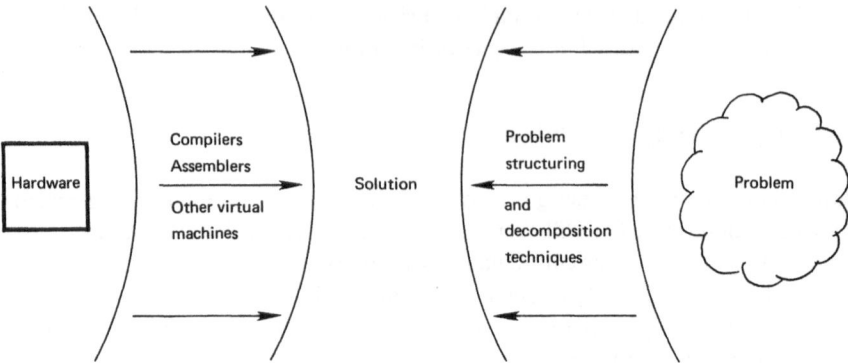

Figure 1.3 Problem vs hardware

Example

Imagine the situation where a scientist wishes to create a simple program to
carry out some calculations. His problem is to design the software to solve
a series of equations and formulae. With no support software to provide a
convenient virtual machine, he must concentrate on translating the equations
into a large number of machine instructions. A problem that can be expressed
conveniently as a few lines of mathematical formulae becomes a complex
problem in machine code.

   If, however, the scientist was presented with a machine that would accept
and implement his problem, stated not as machine instructions but as a mathematical formula, then his task would be greatly simplified. He would not need to
become involved in the detailed machine operation, and the likelihood of error
is thus reduced. More importantly, he is free to concentrate on the problem
itself, rather than the implementation of its software solution. In order that
he may interface with a virtual machine, as opposed to a real machine, a
translating program must be provided to translate the scientist's description
of the problem solution into a form suitable for machine execution. Commonly
this translator exists as a FORTRAN compiler. The scientist can express his
design in the FORTRAN language, to be executed, as far as he is concerned, on
a 'FORTRAN machine'.

   A designer in a business data-processing environment conceives of his
problem in terms of structured data files, movement of data between files and
the generation of reports. The basic hardware is by no means an ideal vehicle
for the solution of his problem. (Nor, in fact, is the scientist's virtual machine,
although it may go some of the way.) The data-processing designer requires a
'business' machine. This form of virtual machine is conventionally provided by
a COBOL or RPG language translator. Figure 1.4 shows the layers of software
providing virtual machines in a commercial environment.

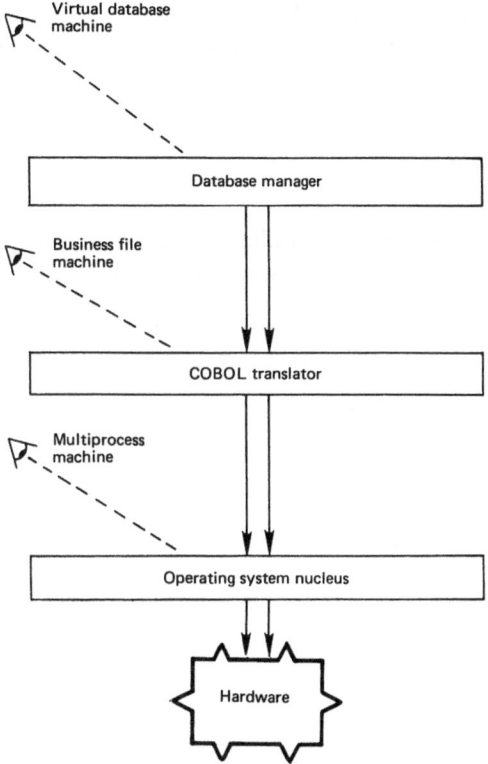

Figure 1.4 Levels of business-orientated virtual machines

If we consider the area of real-time software, it is clear that the designer of a real-time system would be able to utilise a virtual machine tailored to *his* environment. A major benefit would be the reduction in complexity and, therefore, cost of the final design. The virtual machine, not the designer, would take care of the detailed translation into machine code.

1.4 SUMMARY

Most descriptions of real-time software emphasise the need for a rapid response to the environment. In many early systems, this was possibly the sole design criterion. However, as with any product, real-time software must be as correct, complete, reliable and economical as possible. A design that results in fast responsive software is not completely useful unless it employs a strong structure to reduce complexity. Some of the tools and techniques discussed in the following chapters are by no means specific to real-time software, but they must be included in our discussion as they are vital for successful design.

We have already introduced the first of these tools — the virtual machine. Chapters 2 to 5 will discuss a virtual machine designed for use in a real-time environment.

Concepts

Real-time; controlled system; controlling system; batch; on-line; life-cycle cost; maintenance; complexity; structure; virtual machine

2 The Real-time Virtual Machine – Its Properties

We may think of a real-time system as carrying out a set of activities or tasks. Controlling a device could be one activity; keeping a record of the over-all performance of the system may be another. All the activities in the system are interrelated and interact with one another. Some activities may be more vital than others, dependent upon the environmental conditions affecting the controlled system at any one time. Continuous variations in the nature of the environment make it difficult to predict which activities, from a set of possible activities, a real-time system will be required to carry out next. Clearly, a real-time system is multifaceted and exhibits enormous complexity. We are faced with a set of interdependent activities, all jostling to be carried out within strict time limits. Unless some form of abstraction is applied, the design process becomes almost impossible.

A method of attaining this abstraction is to design, create and use a suitable virtual machine. If such a machine can be developed for a real-time environment, then the design problem can be reduced to manageable proportions. This chapter will discuss a virtual machine which provides a useful basis for the design of a real-time system. The form of the machine to be used is strongly influenced by ideas developed in the MASCOT (1979) development system and the UNIX (1978) operating system.

We have already seen that the existence of a virtual machine enables a designer to attain a degree of abstraction from the computer hardware. However, the virtual machine must do more than simply reduce programming complexity. It must be adapted to suit the needs of its environment and area of application. It must be designed in such a way that it facilitates and encourages the creation of clear, logical and easily implemented designs. More, it must promote the design of systems that are as simple as possible.

It is with these criteria in mind that we shall discuss the design of a real-time virtual machine. We shall proceed by considering what facilities a real-time machine would require, and systematically include them in our model. At each stage we shall attempt to ensure that the form of the machine will encourage clean designs of minimum complexity.

2.1 PROCESSES

A real-time system can be seen as one that carries out a set of activities. The most elementary real-time system would, therefore, be one which carried out one, and only one activity. An example of this would be a system that ensures, by controlling a valve, an even flow of fluid in a pipe; note figure 2.1. The activity to be performed by this controlling system is quite straightforward, as is evident in figure 2.2. In order to build such a controlling system it would be

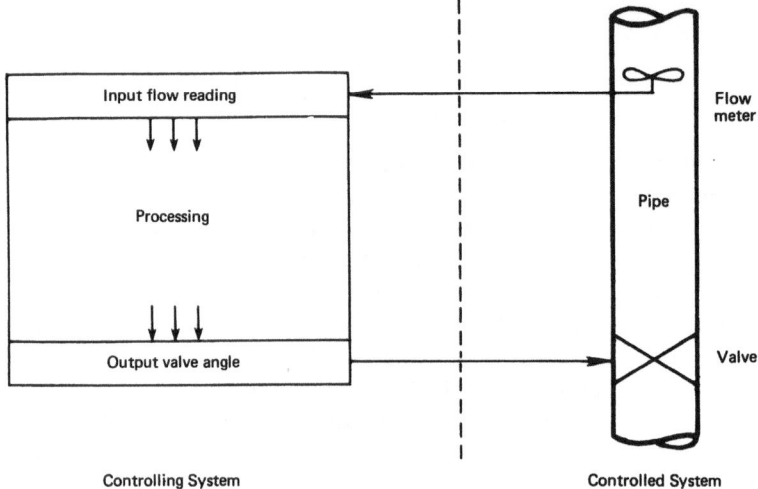

Figure 2.1 Fluid flow control system

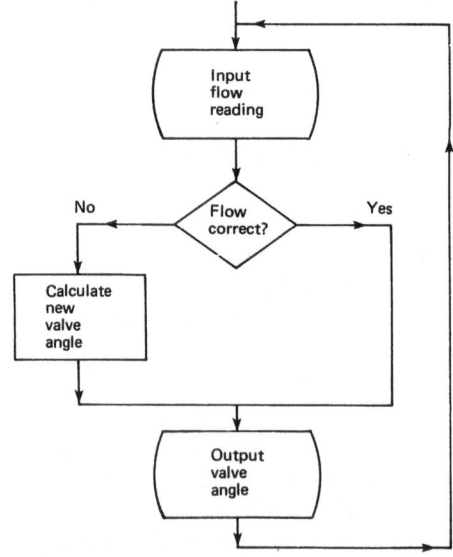

Figure 2.2 Fluid flow processing

necessary to provide a suitable program of instructions, together with the processing hardware on which it could run. We shall call the combination of a simple free-standing program and its processing hardware, which together implement one activity, a *process*. As we refine our virtual machine, so we may need to extend the definition of a process. For the moment, we shall retain the correspondence between an activity that needs to be carried out and the process that carries it out. The simple flow-control system that we have been discussing would consist of one process, as it only carries out one activity. We shall represent a process graphically in the manner used by the MASCOT system, as shown in figure 2.3. In order to specify the process completely, we would need to define precisely what activity the process must carry out, and also its interaction with the outside world.

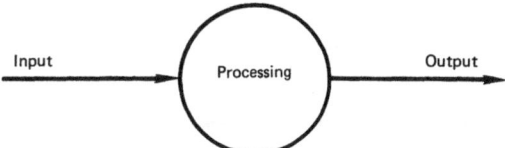

Figure 2.3 Process symbol

Our simple virtual machine will support the existence of a single process. To extend our model further, the real-time system could be asked to perform a number of unrelated activities. Expanding our previous example we could look at a system that controls the flow of fluid in a pipe, the level of grain in a bin, the temperature of a furnace and the level of fluid in a tank.

Here, the pipe, bin, furnace and tank are all part of separate, unrelated machinery, and therefore the activities controlling them will have no effect on one another. As in the previous system, the controlling activities can be implemented as individual processes. The situation is shown in figure 2.4. Since the devices they control are independent, the processes themselves are independent. Since no process depends upon another, they need not co-operate with one another or synchronise their activities in any way. The system design task would simply be that of designing the programs for each process, and providing suitable processing hardware. But out virtual machine must be extended to support as many processes as the designer may require.

It is unlikely that a real-time system would be asked to control a number of totally unrelated devices. Normally, it would be required to control an environment where the devices, and therefore the processes controlling them, are interrelated in some way. Figure 2.5 depicts a hypothetical grain-roasting plant. Now, if the pipe, bin, furnace and tank described in the previous paragraphs were in fact the devices in the grain-roasting plant, then they would form parts of an interrelated system. In this situation the action of one device must take into account the action of the other devices. We are no longer faced with a set of independent processes, and the virtual machine that supports

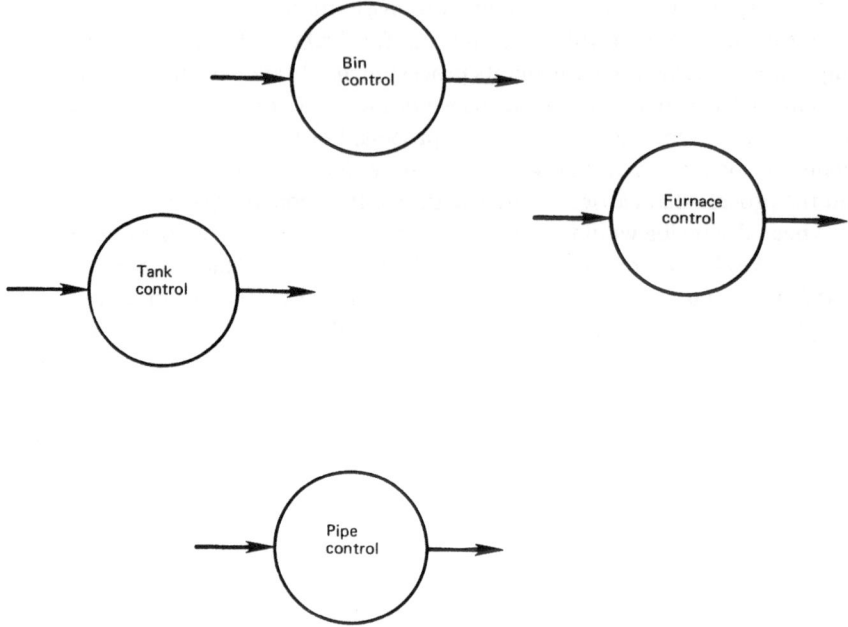

Figure 2.4 Multiple independent processes

multiple but independent processes is no longer adequate. It must be extended
to include *interaction between processes.* In a graphical representation we
could illustrate this interaction with arrows. Where one process wishes to
interact with another, we will draw an arrow between the two processes. If each
process wishes to interact with all the others, then we have a situation as
shown in figure 2.6. Clearly, with more than three or four processes the
situation becomes extremely complex, as can be seen from the confused nature
of the diagram.

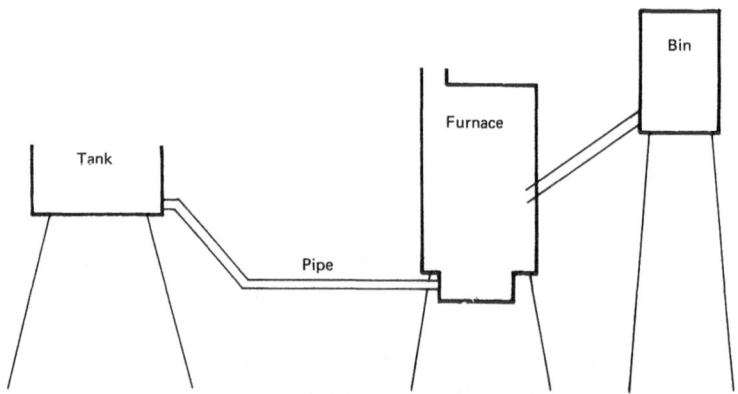

Figure 2.5 Grain-roasting plant

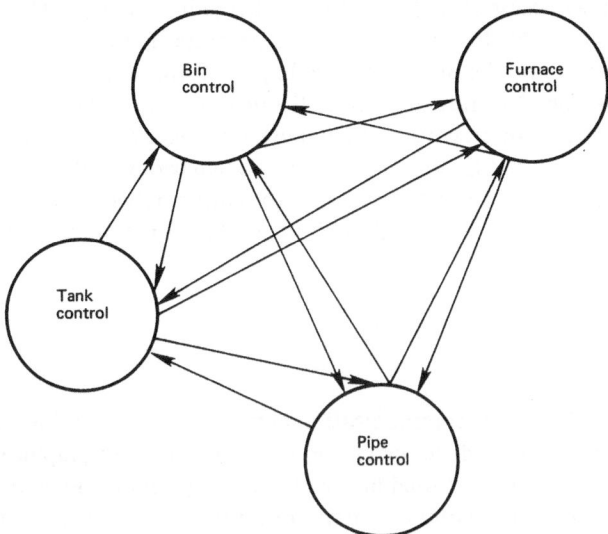

Figure 2.6 Potential process interconnection

If we are to design a worthwhile virtual machine, we must control this complexity. Fortunately, if we give some thought to the way that devices, and therefore processes, wish to interact, we can make a number of abstractions. These abstractions, if applied to the virtual machine, will achieve considerable reduction of the potential complexity.

The interaction of processes will reflect the interaction of the devices they control. This interaction may be direct or immediate, in that the action of one device will cause the starting or stopping of another device's activity. Alternatively, the interaction may be indirect where a device may receive information about the status or actions of another device and be obliged to modify its actions accordingly. The corresponding processes will need to interact in a similar manner. They will need to be able to synchronise their activities, so that the action of one process can cause the activation or suspension of other processes. Also, they will need to be able to send information to one another and to access information that reflects the status of the system as a whole. In order to include the necessary facilities in our virtual machine model, we shall have to discuss process interaction in more detail. The following paragraphs deal with the topics of communication and synchronisation, both vital for successful operation of our virtual machine.

2.2   COMMUNICATION

Information may be communicated between processes in two ways. First, a direct transfer of information may occur from one process to another. Second, each process may access or update pieces of shared information. This shared information is available to some or all of the processes in the system. Recall the grain-roasting system. The process controlling the furnace will send an indication of the required fuel flow rate directly to the process controlling the fuel pipe valve. Meanwhile, both processes may require a knowledge of the current ambient air temperature in order to modify the behaviour of their devices. In the first case we have a direct transfer of information between processes. In the second case, both processes will wish to access a common pool of information.

2.2.1 Channels

In order to provide direct communication between processes in the virtual machine we need to introduce the concept of a *channel*. The graphical representation for a channel used in the MASCOT system is shown in figure 2.7. A channel provides the medium for items of information to be passed between one process and another. A channel has a certain elasticity. More than one item of information can pass through a channel at any one time. Items passing through the channel will usually be ordered so that the first item passed into the channel will be the first item removed at the other end. The virtual machine is unconcerned as to precisely how the transfer of information is effected. It is sufficient in our virtual machine design to say that, where a channel exists between two processes, items of information may flow through that channel from one process to another.

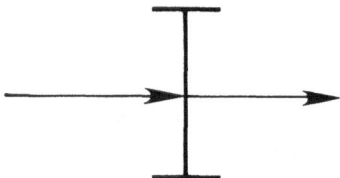

Figure 2.7 The channel

2.2.2 Pools

To provide system-wide information we must introduce another concept to our virtual machine — a *pool*. Items of information in a pool are available for reading and/or writing by a number of processes in the system. Information does not flow within a pool A pool acts as a repository of information; any item in it will be available to processes using the pool. The virtual machine provides no indication as to how the pool will be set up; it simply provides the

Figure 2.8 The pool

facility for specifying that a pool of information does exist. Figure 2.8 illustrates the MASCOT symbol for a pool.

Pools are as important an element in the virtual machine as processes. Whereas processes are software models of the activities that a real-time system must perform, pools form the software models of *items* in the system. These items include physical devices and mechanisms in the controlled system, and conceptual items such as logical files.

Figure 2.9 shows a simple system consisting of five processes communicating via three channels and two pools.

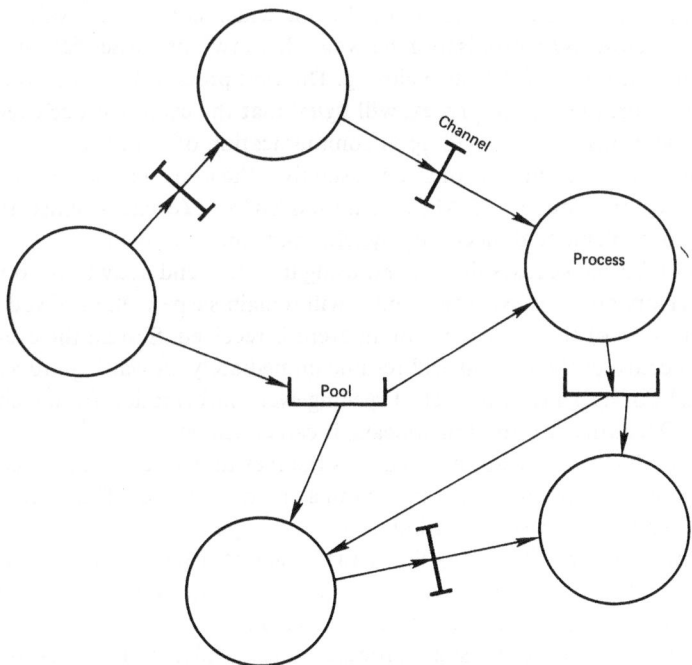

Figure 2.9 Processes, channels and pools

2.3   SYNCHRONISATION

So far we have discussed only half of the complexity problem introduced by
process interaction. As well as communicating information to one another, processes
may wish to synchronise their activities. This synchronisation involves the ability
of one process to stimulate or inhibit its own action or that of other processes.
In other words, in order to carry out the activities required of it, a process may
need to have the ability to say STOP or GO or WAIT A MOMENT to itself, or
other processes.

   If each process has the power to stop or start the activity of any other
process in the system, the complexity shown in the interaction diagram (figure
2.6) will still apply. It is important that a process must *not* be allowed to have
this direct power over other processes. Fortunately, we can design simple
procedures which fulfil all the requirements of interprocess synchronisation and,
at the same time, limit the process-activation and suspension powers of the process
using them.

2.3.1 Significant Events

Interprocess synchronisation centres around the occurrence of significant events
in the system. Consider an example. One process in a system may need to
suspend its activities at a certain point until such time as a valve is closed.
Another process in the system will be the one which controls the valve and
causes it to close. Synchronisation between these two processes centres around
the significant event of the valve closing. The first process must *wait* for the
event to occur; the second process will *signal* that the event has occurred.

   Synchronisation is based upon communication of a piece of information
between processes. This information is simply: 'the event has occurred.'

   If two procedures – WAIT (event) and SIGNAL(event) – exist, they can
be used to implement all necessary synchronisation.

   WAIT(event) causes the process using it to suspend activity as soon as
the WAIT operation is executed, and it will remain suspended until such time
as notification of the occurrence of an event is received. Should the event have
already occurred, the process will resume immediately. A waiting process can
be thought of as being in the act of reading event information from a channel
or pool. Once this information appears, it can continue.

   The SIGNAL operation broadcasts the fact that an event has occurred.
Its action is to place event information in a channel or pool. This in turn may
enable a waiting process to continue.

   The designer, when using the virtual machine, need not be concerned
with how the WAIT and SIGNAL operations are implemented. He is nevertheless
in a position to base the design of process synchronisation on the occurrence of
significant events. He can display process interdependency diagramatically by
showing the channels and pools through which knowledge of the event is
transmitted.

2.3.2 Interrupts

It must be mentioned at this stage that the signalling of an event is not necessarily performed solely by processes within the system. In the previous example, the valve-control process presumably monitored the state of the valve until such time as it closed. At this point, the process signalled the event. The designer may, however, prefer the valve to signal the event directly. We shall display sources of events, external to the software, as squares, shown in figure 2.10. This feature is, in fact, a *hardware interrupt* mechanism, described in more detail in section 4.1. However, the user of the virtual machine need not concern himself with the physical implementation of the mechanism.

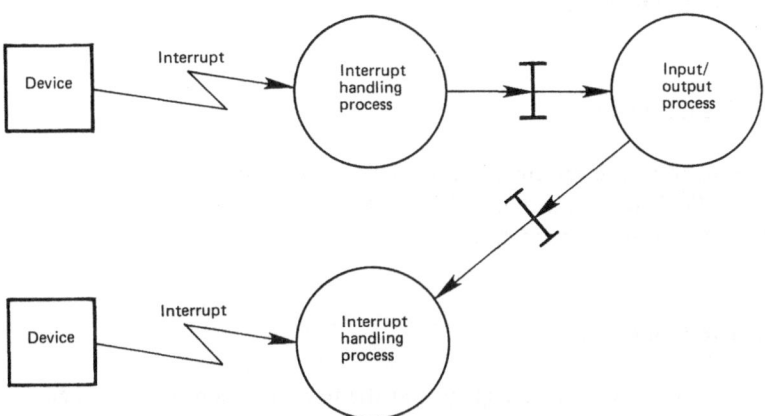

Figure 2.10 External signals – interrupts

2.4   EXAMPLE

In order to illustrate our ideas more clearly, it may be useful to analyse a very simple example. We shall look at a small information system. A number of terminals are attached to a computer system. By using a terminal, a person may interrogate and possibly update information in a set of files held on the computer's backing store. The person must first make himself known to the system by typing in a password. He can then, using a set of one-line commands, read from and, if he is eligible, write to the system files. This arrangement is, of course, a very simple basis for a management information system, stock-control system, airline booking scheme or similar. To start the design for the software needed to control this system we shall identify first the *items* in the system, and then the *activities* that must be carried out.

2.4.1 Items

2.4.1.1 The Users

Each user of the system will have a password, and some security code that
indicates to which files he may read and/or write.

2.4.1.2 The Terminals

In this simple system we will assume that each terminal is allocated a unique
location in the computer's main storage, in which it can place a character as it
is typed. Similarly, there is a unique location where it accesses the next character
to be sent to the terminal.

2.4.1.3 The Commands

Each command to the system will take the form of a line of text and represents
one action. Such actions would include 'read a file record', or 'write a file
record', or 'move to the next record'.

2.4.1.4 The Responses

These will be strings of text, displayed at the terminals as responses to commands.

2.4.1.5 The Files

These are the information files that the users wish to manipulate.

2.4.2 Activities

2.4.2.1 Handle Terminal Input

The system must move characters out of each terminal's input location fast
enough to ensure that no character is overwritten by the next incoming
character. The characters make up commands. Each command consists of a
string of characters terminated by an end-of-line indication. The activity-
handling terminal input will send in characters until an end-of-line character
is received, at which point it will signal that a command has been read.

2.4.2.2 Handle Terminal Output

The system will build responses to the user in the form of strings of characters. We must provide an activity that will place these responses, character by character, into the terminal's output location.

2.4.2.3 File Handler

We need to include an activity to control the organisation and access to the information in the system files.

2.4.2.4 Carry Out Commands

Finally we will interpret the user commands. We must ensure that the user and/ or the command is valid and legal, then take action on the command and provide a response to the user.

2.4.3 The Design

Every *item* in the system will be modelled as a *pool*. Every *activity* will be modelled as a *process*. One possible design is shown in figure 2.11. A terminal is in fact two devices, the keyboard for input and the screen or printer for output.

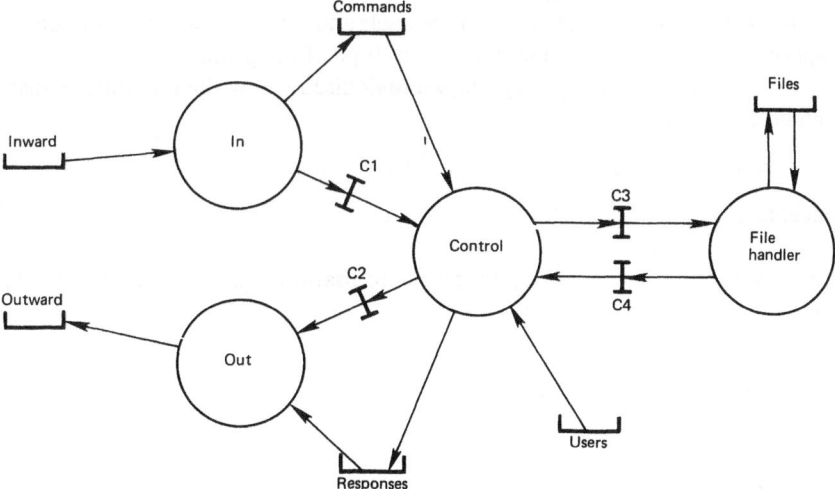

Figure 2.11 Possible design for information system

The IN process builds up commands, character by character, in the COMMAND pool. When it receives and end-of-line indicator, it sends a message down C1, indicating that a command has been received. When the OUT process receives a message down C2, it transfers the response specified by the message to the terminal output location. When signalled by IN, the control process checks the validity of the command by referring to the USERS pool to check user passwords and security codes. It then sends a request for action by the file handler down C3. It receives an acknowledgement to this request on C4. It then places the response to the command in RESPONSES and signals OUT.

Thus, we build up an initial, broad software design, modelling the items as pools, activities as processes and communication synchronisation as channels.

2.5 SUMMARY

At this stage the virtual machine is sufficiently well defined to be used as a system design tool. The system of co-operating processes closely parallels the system of interrelated activities that must be performed by a real-time system. At the top level of his design, the designer produces:

(1) a description of the system pools;
(2) a description of the basic process activities;
(3) a chart of the interrelationship between the system elements showing channel and pool access indicators.

Next he tackles the internal design of the processes themselves. The current form of the real-time virtual machine simplifies this task. Each process can be designed as if it were the only process in the system. Its interfaces with the outside world are defined in terms of channels and pools. It can therefore be designed as if it were a free-standing 'batch' type of program.

In the following three chapters, we shall discuss how the real-time virtual machine can be created.

Concepts

Activities; processes; channels; pools; synchronisation; significant event; WAIT; SIGNAL; interrupt

3 Implementing the Real-time Machine

It would appear that the real-time virtual machine described in chapter 2 should provide the software designer with a useful working environment. This chapter will describe the software and hardware necessary to support the existence of such a virtual machine. It will be necessary to implement processes, and to provide communication and synchronisation facilities between the processes.

A *process* consists of a processor, program code and sufficient memory to accommodate this program code. We must produce a machine that provides these resources for as many processes as the designer sees fit. Each process must, as far as the process itself is concerned, have its own processor (CPU), program and memory. We can provide these resources by either dedicating unique resources to each process or by sharing the available resources between the processes.

3.1 IMPLEMENTING PROCESSES – DEDICATED RESOURCES

The recent availability of cheap microprocessors and memory elements means that it is a viable proposition to provide separate resources dedicated to each process. It is possible to provide for each process in the system a separate microprocessor, together with enough memory for the code element. If the designer specifies a new process, a new CPU/memory is slotted into the system.

Figures 3.1 and 3.2 illustrate, schematically, two commonly used configurations of multiprocessor hardware. In figure 3.1 the microprocessors use their own local memory to store program code. They communicate with one another via communications links that are set up to allow relatively long distances between the CPU/memory modules. There is a clear correspondence between the channels of the virtual machine and the physical links between the microprocessor modules.

Figure 3.2 shows processors connected via a common bus arrangement. The local storage for each CPU may contain all or some of the process code. If the local memory does not contain all of the program code for a process, then some will be held in shared memory. The shared memory is the logical place to hold the information in the system pools.

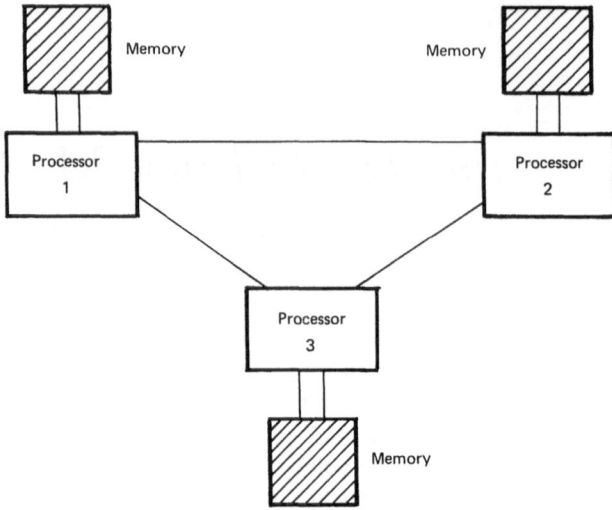

Figure 3.1 Distributed processor arrangement 1

With either of the above configurations it is clear that we are in a position to provide a CPU/memory/code combination for each process. In order to create a process one need only load one of the memory modules with the relevant program code element. Clearly this simple and elegant approach should be utilised wherever feasible. It has, however, a number of drawbacks in certain circumstances.

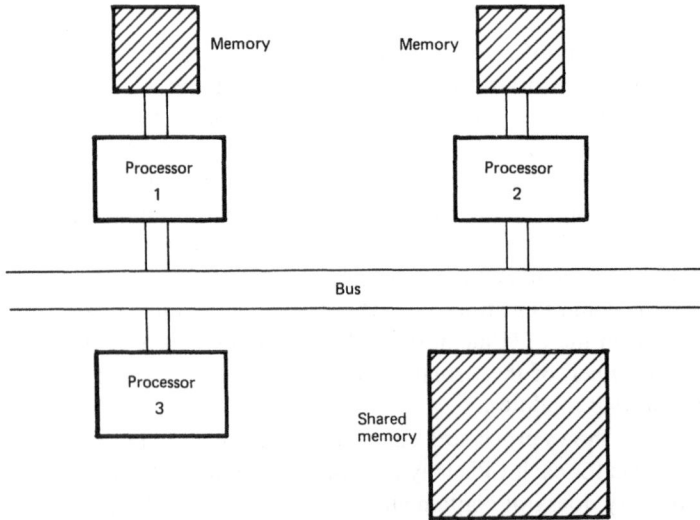

Figure 3.2 Distributed processor arrangement 2

(1) Cost

Frequently, economic constraints rule out the possibility of providing a unique CPU/memory module for each process. If insufficient resources are available, it becomes necessary to share resources between processes. None the less, in applications requiring a small, fixed number of processes, with modest reliability requirements, the simple multimicroprocessor realisation of the virtual machine would be the most desirable configuration.

(2) Lack of Flexibility

There are more compelling reasons for introducing a more flexible relationship between processes and their hardware resources. A rigid allocation of process to CPU/memory implies that no new processes can be introduced into the system without altering the hardware configuration. In some applications this can prove a severe restriction. Some systems may require that the number of processes in the system vary with the workload on the system. A fixed CPU allocation would imply that the number of processes in the system is constant. This would severely impinge on possible expansion. The system could not be extended to include new activities without adding further hardware.

(3) Reliability

Considerations of system reliability make it convenient to include redundant CPU and memory modules in the system. When a piece of hardware fails, the system can be reconfigured to use the redundant standby modules. This technique is difficult to employ if there is a rigid allocation of process to CPU/memory. We shall discuss system reliability in some detail in chapter 5.

3.2 IMPLEMENTING PROCESSES – SHARED RESOURCES

3.2.1 Sharing the Processor

When discussing the ways in which a CPU (or CPUs less in number than all the processes) may be shared among the processes, it is necessary to consider three factors

(1) *how* the CPU is to be shared – in other words, what mechanisms are required to enable a processor executing the code element of one process to change its activity and execute the code element of another process;

(2) *when* the CPU is to be shared – that is, at what times, or as a result of

what events, should the CPU change from executing one process to
executing another;

(3) *which* process should the CPU direct its attention to, when sharing of the
CPU is necessary.

Points (1) and (2) — *how* and *when* — we shall discuss in the following sections;
point (3) — *which* process — we shall leave to chapter 4, where we discuss
process scheduling.

3.2.1.1 Serial Execution

The simplest method of sharing a CPU is for the processes to be executed once
through their code without interruption, one process after another.

This method causes the system to lose its responsiveness to environmental
changes. It can only change the current process and thus its effect on the environment at the end of execution of the current process. The processes must of
necessity be brief if the controlled system is to remain unaware of the fact
that the processes are not running in parallel. If only one CPU is in use, the
processes must not execute synchronising **WAIT** operations since, clearly, no
other process can run to execute the corresponding **SIGNAL** operation.

Provided the application lends itself to short processes that carry out
highly independent activities, then the simplicity of the serial approach has
much to commend it. *How* is simple in this case: commence the next process
at its starting point. Each process, when terminating, executes a piece of code
that performs this function. And *when*? At the completion of the current process.

3.2.1.2 Pseudoparallel Execution

The major drawback of the serial method occurs when processes take
considerable time to execute, and the system therefore becomes very sluggish
in its response to changes in the environment.

Ideally, in order to react to a change in the controlled system, it should
be possible for a CPU to swap from one process to another at any time, giving
the impression to the environment that the processes are being conducted in
parallel. To make this possible we introduce the concepts of *volatile
environment*, *process descriptor* and *dispatcher*.

Volatile environment   A process's volatile environment is that information that,
if lost, would mean that the process could not continue from the point at which
it last executed an instruction. It is the information that would be lost if
another process used the CPU. The volatile environment includes such
information as the contents of hardware registers, memory-management
registers and the program counter. While the process is running on a CPU, the

volatile environment is continually changing. If the process is denied the use of the CPU for a period, while the CPU is required by another process, then the first process's volatile environment must be preserved. If this is not done the process will be unable to continue from where it left off. If this *is* done and the information is restored to the registers, then the process will be unaware that it ever had anything but total use of the CPU.

Process descriptor   We must therefore, provide a place to store a process's volatile environment while it is not using the CPU. At the same time, we could provide space for summary information about the process for system 'housekeeping' purposes. This storage element will take the form of a data structure that, in effect, models the process. We shall call this data structure a *process descriptor* (PD). So, as a further extension of the *process* concept we could state that the software element of a process consists of a process descriptor and the program code itself; see figure 3.3. The software elements that make up process A in this diagram consist of the left-hand process descriptor and code element. The significance of element S will be discussed in section 3.2.2.1.

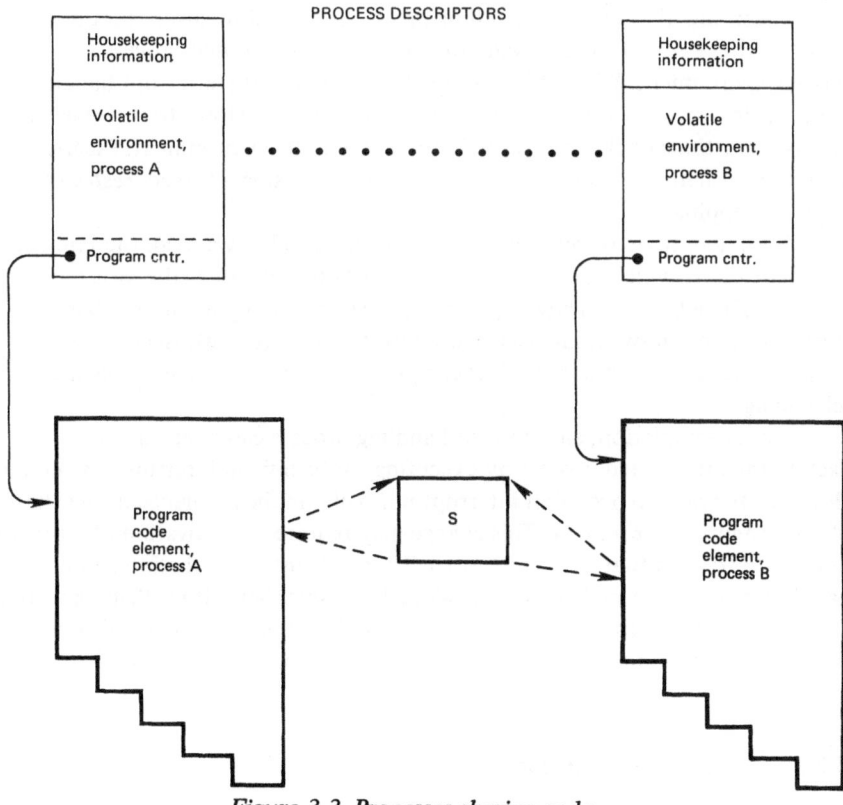

Figure 3.3 Processes sharing code

Dispatcher   The dispatcher is the mechanism that effects the *how* of process sharing. It can be implemented in hardware or software. When activated it stores, in the relevant process descriptor, the contents of the hardware registers that make up the volatile environment of the currently active process. It then replaces the contents of the registers with volatile environment information from another process's process descriptor.

Release of the CPU   The *when* of process sharing is related to the conditions necessary for the current process to give up use of the processor. A process may relinquish the use of the CPU voluntarily, or be forced to do so. A voluntary release of the CPU would occur when a process either terminates or executes an unsuccessful WAIT operation. A forced release of the CPU occurs when an interrupt occurs and an interrupt handling process is activated.

Interrupt handlers   The controlled system commands the attention of the software system by means of the hardware interrupt mechanism. Should an interrupt occur, the hardware saves a portion of the current volatile environment (including at least the program counter) in a fixed location and replaces it with the volatile environment of the process designed to handle the interrupt. When executing, the interrupt handling process is careful to ensure that it does not affect any of the unsaved portions of the interrupted process's volatile environment. When it has completed its action, the interrupt handler can execute a return-from-interrupt instruction, which restores to the registers the saved portions of the interrupted process's volatile environment. Clearly, the interrupt hardware acts as a simple dispatcher causing a forced, *restricted* process swapping.

Note here that, as well as forcing the process to be swapped, the interrupt specifies exactly which process will subsequently be activated (the interrupt handler). The *when* and *which* aspects of process swapping are indivisible concepts when the swapping occurs as a result of an interrupt. Accordingly, we shall further our discussion of interrupts in section 4.1, when discussing scheduling.

On its completion, an interrupt handling process can swap the processor back to the interrupted process by executing a return-from-interrupt instruction. However, the occurrence of an interrupt normally implies a change in the status of the system's environment. This change may require the activation of a process other than the one that was interrupted. Thus, it is usual for the interrupt handling process to terminate by signalling the dispatcher, rather than executing a return-from-interrupt instruction. The dispatcher then finds which process should run next and effects the necessary swapping of complete volatile environments.

3.2.2 Sharing the Main Memory

If we assume that one CPU can be shared between more than one process, it remains necessary to provide main memory to hold the process code elements. The simplest way, and the one to be used if possible, is to provide in the system enough memory for each process to have its own unique area. Often this simple expedient cannot be employed. In most modern systems the cost of main memory far outweighs the cost of the CPU. For many systems the high cost of main memory will force a reduction of main memory capacity. This implies that the available memory must be shared between the processes in the system.

There are two ways of effecting memory sharing – to share the code that resides in a section of memory, or to share the use of the section of memory itself. Let us consider the simpler method first.

3.2.2.1 Code Sharing

Real-time systems frequently contain a number of actions that form part of more than one process in the system. Conventionally, these activities are implemented as subroutines and a copy is built into the code element of any process that needs it. Now, if one of these subroutines were of any considerable size, a great saving in memory space could be achieved if the processes could share the code of the common routine, rather than each having a copy.

A program or subroutine consists of instructions plus data. Therefore, the shared routine will have local storage areas for its temporary working variables. In a shared CPU environment a process may be forced to give up the processor at any time during its execution. So, in figure 3.3 process A may be half way through executing routine S when it gives up the processor. Process B then takes over the processor and enters routine S. While S is executed, the temporary data in S will be manipulated according to B's requirements. If A then regains use of the processor, the temporary data used in S will have been changed by B's action. This fact is unknown to A and may cause it to malfunction.

There are two ways of avoiding this situation, as follows.

(a) Serially re-useable code   One method is to write the code in subroutine S in such a way that it makes no assumptions about the values in its local variables when it is entered. In other words, the initial values of the local data have no effect on the routine's action. Usually, the first action of the subroutine would be to set its local variables to a fixed, initial set of values. If a lock mechanism is applied at the beginning of the subroutine, and an unlock at the end, such that only one process may be executing its code at any one time, then processes can safely use the code, one after the other. The code is serially re-usable. The lock and unlock mechanisms can be implemented easily using WAIT and SIGNAL operations. The use of these operations to ensure serial access to code segments is discussed further in section 3.8.

(b) Re-entrant or pure code   If all the temporary data areas needed by S were to be part of the process currently using S, rather than part of S itself, then S

would consist of executable code only. Therefore, it could be executed by more than one process at a time, provided that S did not modify its own instructions in any way. Code elements having this property are referred to as re-entrant or pure procedures.

If a piece of re-entrant code is to act on different data areas, which are dependent on the process using it, it must access this data in an indirect manner. Typically, the re-entrant code module will access the data via a relocation pointer which is associated with each process. This relocation pointer containing the address of the beginning of the process data could be passed as a parameter when the subroutine is called.

Each process will call the re-entrant subroutine by transferring control to the start of the routine. Some mechanisms will be needed to store the return address of the subroutine call. This is supplied conveniently by a stack mechanism. A stack can be regarded as a last-in-first-out queue of memory elements. The stack area must be part of the individual processes. In some implementations, the local data area is also included as part of the stack.

The amount of shared code that a process uses could be extended to include the whole of the process's code. In figure 3.4 there are a number of processes that execute the same code. They are, however, completely different processes because they use different data areas. Note that each process sees itself as consisting of its data together with its own code area. It is unaware, and unconcerned, that another process is actually using part of the same code for its action.

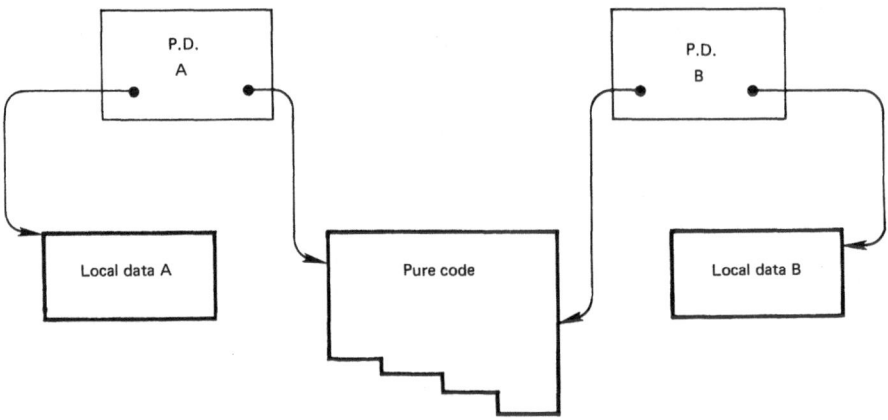

Figure 3.4 Different processes, same code element

The device drivers in a conventional operating system are a good example of this situation. When building an operating system's facilities it is usual to include input/output processes to handle idiosyncracies of the different devices attached to the system. Figure 3.5 shows such a situation displayed as processes in the virtual machine. Now, to implement device-handler processes

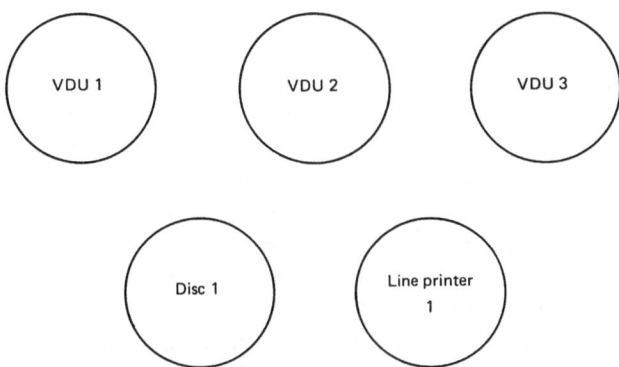

Figure 3.5 Input/output drivers

the systems programmer constructs the data structures and code modules
shown in figure 3.6 The device descriptors contain device-specific information
such as character set and speed. The device driver code uses the information in
the device descriptors to tailor its actions. The device driver code, process
descriptor, plus a device descriptor constitutes a process. To introduce a new
process to handle another terminal, for example, the systems programmer need
only create another device descriptor and process descriptor.

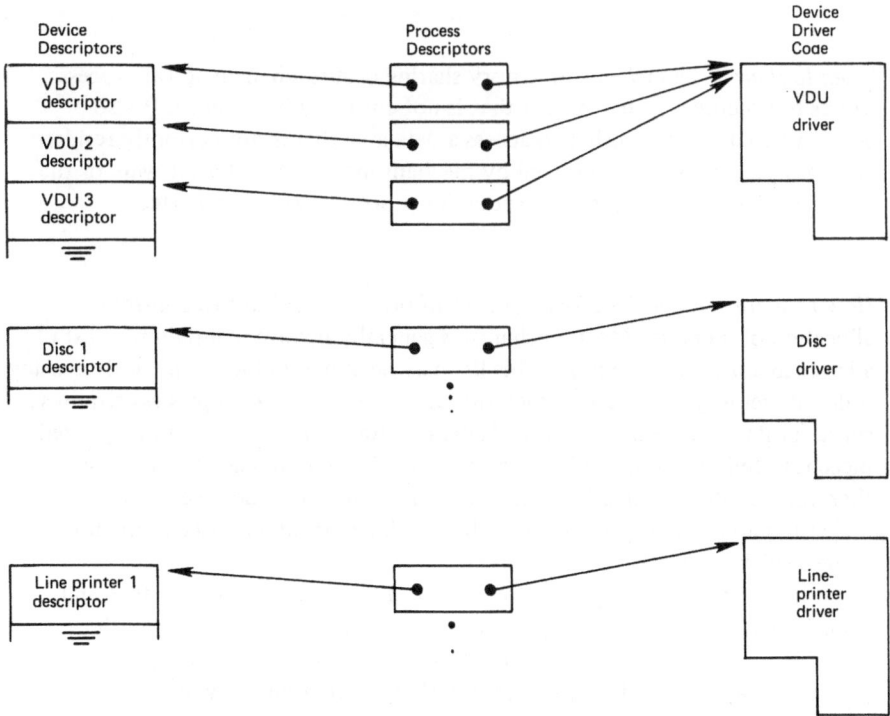

Figure 3.6 Input/output-driver data structures

3.2.2.2 Memory Sharing

Even with extensive use of code sharing it will not always be possible simultaneously to accommodate all the process code in main memory. In this instance it will be necessary to hold code and data elements that are not currently being executed on a storage medium of higher capacity than the main storage. This medium, referred to as backing store, typically takes the form of magnetic discs and drums. Backing store is cheaper per unit of storage but slower to access than main storage. Code elements will be held on backing store and copied to main storage when it becomes necessary to execute them. If a copy of a code element is currently in main storage, it is *resident* and may be executed immediately; if not, it is *non-resident* and must be copied to main storage before it can be executed by the CPU.

    Most real-time systems divide main memory into two areas. The first holds frequently executed code elements and the code elements of highly time-critical processes. These code elements reside permanently in memory. The second area is set aside as a free space to be shared between the remaining code in the system. These remaining elements consist of processes that are less time-critical in nature and code that is less frequently executed. The relative size of the two areas will depend upon the requirements and constraints of the particular system.

When to share   The *when* of memory sharing occurs when an active process wishes to execute a code segment that is not currently in memory. It also occurs when a process wishes to access a data area that is not currently resident in memory. This event is detected by mechanisms in either the software or the hardware. The memory-sharing process, or processes, are then alerted.

How to share   A special process, or set of processes, is built to control the allocation of memory. Most mechanisms generally involve maintaining a list of all available pieces of memory. This list may be sorted in increasing or decreasing order of memory piece size or memory piece address. When a process requires space for its code element a search is made through this list. If a suitably sized piece is found, it is allocated to that process. The required code element is then copied into this area from backing store. Once this code section is no longer required it may be copied to the backing store and a piece of memory made available for other processes.

    If a higher-priority process requests a large piece of memory store and finds it unavailable, a shuffler process may be called on to coalesce all the available free memory space. If this proves inadequate, then lower-priority processes may be called on to relinquish their current memory allocation, allowing the high-priority process room to run.

3.3 IMPLEMENTING SYNCHRONISATION

Many different synchronisation facilities or functions can be thought to be useful. They include DELAYME(time), ACTIVATE(other process), SUSPEND(other process) and DELAY(other process, time). DELAYME can be implemented as a WAIT on an event that will occur 'time' later. Facilities like ACTIVATE, SUSPEND and DELAY are dangerous. Their existence implies that the affected processes do not have total control of their synchronisation activities.

In fact, all necessary synchronisation activities can be implemented using WAIT and SIGNAL. The detailed implementation of WAIT and SIGNAL depends on the system involved. At the lowest level they rely on a hardware lock-and-unlock mechanism to ensure that they are impervious to process swapping while they take action. At a high level they may be embedded in high-level language constructs.

3.3.1 Semaphores

Dijkstra (1968) has outlined a synchronisation concept against which other methods are measured. He introduced the idea of a *semaphore*, a simple data item that can only take non-negative integer values and can only be manipulated by three procedures: *initialise(semaphore, value)*, *wait(semaphore)* and *signal(semaphore)*. *Initialise* sets the value of the semaphore to *value*. *Signal* simply increments the value of the semaphore by one. *Wait* will decrease the value of the semaphore by one, but only if the result is non-negative.

Processes wishing to synchronise their activities execute *wait* and *signal* operations on shared semaphores. If a process executes a *wait* operation and the value of the semaphore is one or greater, then the process can decrement the semaphore and continue. If, however, the semaphore has the value zero at the time the process executes the *wait* operation, then decrementing the semaphore would result in a negative value. The process must therefore wait until such time as another process executes a *signal* operation in the semaphore, thus allowing the first process to decrement the semaphore and continue.

At any time, the value of the semaphore is equal to its initial value *plus* the number of *signal* operations that have been applied to it *minus* the total number of completed (that is, passed) *wait* operations. Now, because the value of a semaphore can never be negative, this implies that the number of completed *wait* operations on a semaphore must always be less than or equal to the initial value of the semaphore plus the number of *signal* operations that have occurred.

Both *wait* and *signal* are indivisible operations; once begun, they must be completed. The processor cannot be swapped while they are being executed. This stipulation ensures that the vital incrementing and decrementing of the semaphore occurs without interruption. Examples of the implementation and use of semaphores are given in section 3.8

If we were to use semaphores as the synchronising agency in our real-time machine, then the significant event (see section 2.3) would be the incrementing of the semaphore. The semaphores themselves would reside in pools, monitored by the *wait* and *signal* operations.

A *software trap* is a machine instruction that, when executed, causes an interrupt to be signalled to the interrupt mechanism. It is an interrupt generated by software. It is worth noting that, if *wait* and *signal* operations are implemented in such a way that they are entered as a result of a software trap, then they are in fact interrupt handling processes. The dispatcher will be activated on their completion.

3.4   IMPLEMENTING COMMUNICATION

In order to facilitate communication between processes, information available to one process must be made available to another process. This implies that an item of information stored in one area of the system's memory, accessible by one process, must be made accessible to other processes. This means that either the data is copied to another area of memory, or the same area of memory is available to all processes wishing to communicate.

In the discussion that follows, 'memory' will refer to both main storage and backing store. For the software designer the framework and principles remain the same; economics and performance requirements will govern his decision as to the location of data. Main memory can be accessed quickly, but more information can be placed on backing store. If large amounts of information are to be shared between processes then files on backing store would be most appropriate. If, however, real-time constraints make slow information access unacceptable, more expensive main storage will have to be used. The data itself must be unaffected by the location of memory storage. A data pool may be located on backing store or in main memory. Only the access procedures vary. The rapid advance in storage technology and the continual decrease in hardware costs makes it vital to keep the data independent of the storage location. Unless the data structure is independent of the storage technology, it will not be possible for the designer to adapt the design to changing hardware economics.

3.4.1 The Channel

The purpose of the channel is to provide a pipe of information passing from one process to another. As well as providing a vehicle for communication, it provides an elastic link between processes within the system. For the processes to run truly asynchronously there must be some buffering of information; the larger the buffers, the greater the system flexibility.

The information to be passed from one process to another is best designed as a fixed-format message. It will usually contain identification information such as the name of the sending process. The message may contain the data itself, or it may be a pointer to the data. Commonly either of two mechanisms are used to carry the message, the *queue* or the *hopper.*

3.4.1.1 The Queue

A widely used form of channel implementation is the first-in-first-out (FIFO) queue. Here, messages are placed on the tail of the queue by the sending process and removed from the head of the queue by the receiving process. Figure 3.7 illustrates this arrangement. Note that when a parcel of information is to be passed between processes a message must be built by writing information to a section of storage. This storage is obtained from an available system freespace area. When a receiving process finishes with the transmitted information, it will return the storage element to the system freespace.

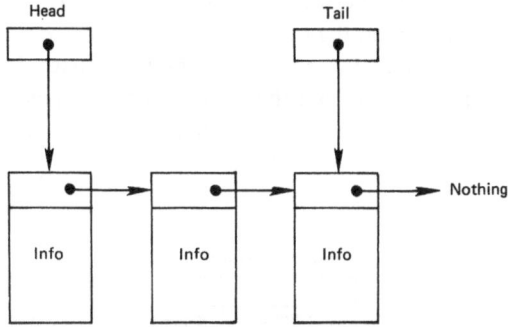

Figure 3.7 The queue

A distributed processor arrangment complicates the situation only slightly. In this case, the implementation of a channel requires the provision of a communication circuit with its associated driving software. The queue is in three pieces. One piece is in the sender's memory awaiting transmission, another is in transit and the other is in the receiver's memory.

The queue need not necessarily have a FIFO organisation. Messages could be given priorities and placed in priority order within the queue. Alternatively, certain sending processes could be given priority, and their messages always placed at the front of the queue.

When queues are operating there is always the possibility that they will grow to the extent that the system freespace will become exhausted. Steps can be taken to avoid this situation. For example, processes with excessively long input queues could be given a high priority (see chapter 4). However, in an overload situation, the available freespace may still become dangerously low. There are two ways around this situation. The system could refuse further work — that is, refuse requests from its controlled system for action. For example, the system controlling an airline booking system could refuse to process any new transactions until an overload was reduced.

Many systems, however, are not in a position to ignore their environment. A second solution to the overload problem is to allow the system freespace to expand into the backing store (if present). Once the freespace in main memory is exhausted, the queue would start using a freespace area on fast backing store.

3.4.1.2 The Hopper

An alternative channel mechanism is a hopper or circular buffer. A fixed-sized buffer is set between the communicating processes. The storage is divided into a number of 'message'-sized elements. The buffer acts as a hopper, see figure 3.8. The transmitting process uses and moves the 'loading' pointer, while the receiving process uses and moves the 'unloading' pointer.

The queue mechanism has the advantage that it can be extended for as long as there are package-sized elements of storage available in the system's freespace area. The hopper, on the other hand, is of fixed size, and this reduces its flexibility. However, it can be manipulated faster than the queue mechanism, as transfers to and from the system freespace area are not required. The decision as to which mechanism is used depends on system performance requirements.

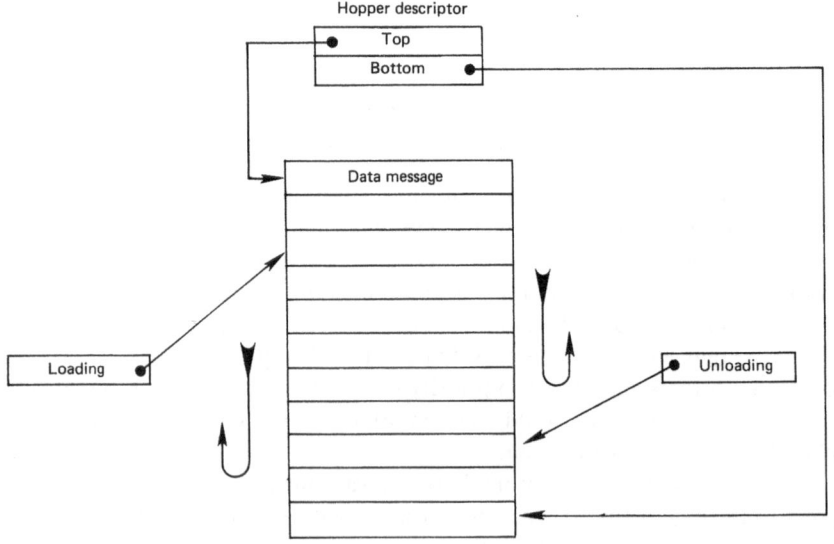

Figure 3.8 The hopper

3.4.2 The Pool

Pools usually take the form of system tables, shared data areas and shared files. In general, they consist of a piece of main memory or backing store which can be read from, or written to, by more than one process. They are used to store information that is relevant to more than one process in the system. The format of the data within the pools will depend on the particular application. They normally consist of data structures which model items in the controlled system or in the software system itself.

The data structures will take the form of tables, lists or individual storage elements held in main memory. In on-line commercial systems, for example, the pools will consist of on-line data files or a centralised database. These files will be read and written to by the processes controlling the on-line terminal activities and transaction processing. Often, for system security and recovery purposes, a regularly updated copy of this information will be held on backing store.

It is essential to control strictly the access to information in pools. If a large number of processes have direct access to a particular pool, a malfunction in one of the processes will cause corruption of pool information, and this will have ramifications throughout the system. Similarly, if any change is made to the format of pool information during the maintenance phase of the product's lifetime, the code for all the processes using the pool will have to be changed. These problems come about if processes using the pool are aware of layout details for the data structures in the pool. Usually, the processes do not need to know this detailed format information, as they are only interested in the data itself. If this is the case, we can introduce the concept of a pool 'policeman' or *monitor.* If a process wishes to access a piece of information in a pool, it does not go to the pool directly, but asks the pool's monitor to carry out the access. It will become evident that this concept of a monitor can be extended to channels and, in fact, to any item in the system.

3.5 MONITORS

While discussing channels and pools we have assumed that implementation of a data structure (queue, file, etc.) is sufficient to fulfil the communication requirements of our virtual machine. In fact, more is required.

Processes should be unaware of the mechanisms driving the channel or pool. They should only need to present the channel or pool with information, or to request information from the channel or pool, and then expect that correct action will be taken. Furthermore, the processes should have no knowledge of the internal workings of the channel or pool. Unless this is the case, the processes will have to know too much about their environment for them to be regarded as free-standing programs.

In the simplest case, we could provide the necessary facilities by creating a number of shared, re-entrant subroutines to be called by the processes. These access procedures would effect the necessary information transfers and, by suitable use of WAIT and SIGNAL operations, ensure that processes did not corrupt the channel or pool data structures. This type of data corruption is all too possible if asynchronous processes are allowed to manipulate common data.

We shall refer to this collection of controlling routines as a *monitor*. When a process wishes to read or write to a channel or pool, it asks the relevant monitor to do the reading or writing for it. Only the monitor is aware of the internal structure of the channel or pool.

Any changes — for example, from a queue mechanism to a hopper mechanism — need only be made known to the monitor. The user processes are unaware, and unconcerned. In this way, processes can be regarded as free-standing programs that utilise communication 'pipes' to interface with the outside world. We shall restrict our definition of a monitor to 'a collection of controlling routines'. Hoare (1974) has proposed a more formalised definition that includes the implementation in a high-level language of modules specifically declared as monitors.

3.5.1 Monitor Facilities

Monitors can be designed to provide increasing levels of service to a real-time system.

3.5.1.1 Basic Facilities

At its simplest, a monitor consists of a group of routines designed to implement the functions of its channel or pool. To do this, it must (a) provide the necessary data-transfer facilities, and (b) ensure adequate synchronisation of the user processes to avoid data corruption.

3.5.1.2 Watchdog Facilities

A monitor can be designed to act as a watchdog or policeman over the activities of its user process. The monitor can check the validity of the information passing through it. In a system test situation, the monitor could cause irregularities to be flagged. In an in-service environment, the monitor could instigate appropriate recovery action if invalid data was being generated by one of its user processes. We shall encounter further examples of monitor watchdog activities as our discussion progresses.

3.5.1.3 Testing/Debugging Facilities

Monitors provide ideal agencies in a system-testing environment or 'test harness'. As they control the flow of information and act as the links between processes, they provide ideal points for inserting software test 'probes', and introducing test data.

Monitors can be built to include all of the above-mentioned facilities. When they are to be used in a time-stringent environment all bar the basic facilities can be removed from the monitors by conditional compilation.

3.6 EXECUTIVE PROCESSES

Various 'special' processes have been mentioned: these include the interrupt-handling process, the process for swapping volatile environments and monitors. All these activities are needed to support the existence of the real-time virtual machine, and fall under the heading of *executive processes*. The executive may be regarded as that part of the real-time system which supports the existence, and controls the activity, of the processes in the system.

Processes that make use of the executive we will call *user processes*. The form and power of the services provided by the executive vary according to the size of the system being constructed. Typically they include: process swapping, interrupt handling, memory allocation, scheduling, interface monitoring, input/output device drivers and file-system control.

A user process, when it wants an executive service, calls on the executive to carry out the required actions. This call could be a simple subroutine call. However, it is desirable to isolate and protect the executive from the possible malfunctions of other processes in the system. The executive will normally be small and consist of highly reliable pieces of code. If the executive is corrupted in any way, it is difficult for the system to continue operation. However, if an individual user process becomes faulty, it may be possible for the executive to take some corrective action.

3.6.1 Protection

In order that no rogue process can corrupt the executive it is desirable to build a 'firewall' between the executive processes and other processes in the system. This protection is not always possible in a very simple microprocessor system. However, most modern minicomputer systems and the more powerful micro-processor systems include some form of memory-management hardware that does allow certain processes greater privileges than others, and does guarantee that processes cannot interfere with the memory allocated to other processes.

Each process is allocated a *protection domain*. A protection domain is the combination of the area of memory in which the process runs and the privileges – such as the ability to execute certain subsets of processor instructions – that the process possesses. Only the most privileged processes are given the power to transfer control of execution to another process's memory area. A simple protection set-up is a two-level 'kernel' and 'user' hierachy. Processes in the kernel domain, or 'kernel space' would have access to all available machine instructions, while processes in user space would be restricted in the set of instructions they would execute.

Now, if memory-management and protection hardware is available to the system, the executive processes will be placed in a privileged area. This arrangement implies that a user process cannot obtain executive service by means of a simple subroutine call. The executive will be situated in a different protection domain, separate from the requesting process. A conventional solution to this problem is for the user process to execute a software trap instruction, after having placed suitable parameters in a location known and available to the executive processes.

The interrupt handling process will then recognise the trap as a call to the executive (system call) and signal to the relevant executive service process. Figure 3.9 shows this arrangement. Note that the executive is always entered via the interrupt service routine (or other closely guarded gateway). The executive is exited via the dispatcher.

It is important that the software designer make full use of the protection mechanisms made available by the hardware. Some hardware systems provide more than two protection domains. If this is the case, then the designer would arrange to place the different processes and executive subroutines in suitable protection domains.

If no protection hardware is available, then a small amount of protection could be afforded by having the process call an executive monitor which checks the legality of the request, rather than calling the executive routines directly.

3.7   BUILDING THE SYSTEM

3.7.1 Bootstrap

Before we arrive at a fully operating real-time system we must build and test the software. In fact, at the outset, we must be capable of loading the process code elements into memory. The usual method is to employ a bootstrap technique. A small program consisting of a very few instructions is permanently stored in a non-erasable section of main storage. The purpose of this program is to load into memory a small process that is itself designed to load the system executive.

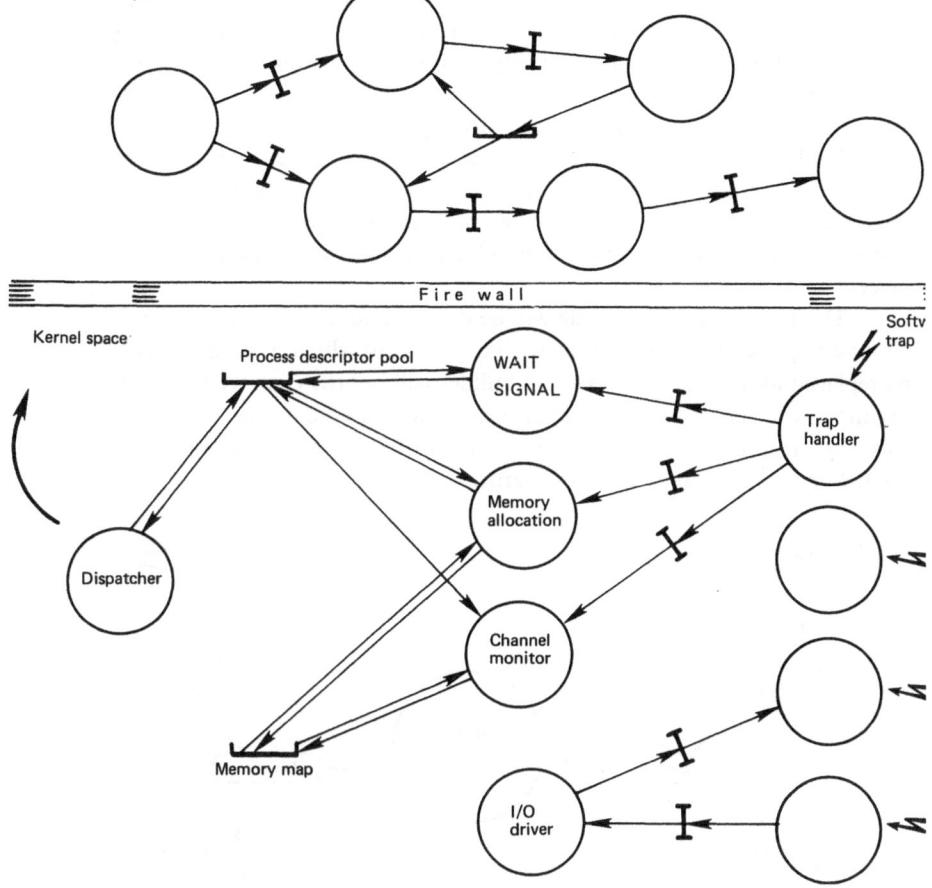

Figure 3.9 Some executive processes

3.7.2 System Builder

Assuming that the executive has been successfully loaded we need to have yet
another executive process. This process, the *system builder*, will be used to
load the code elements of user processes and include their process descriptors
in the process descriptor pool. A description of the system, including data
on the process/channel/pool interconnections, location of code elements and
location of data elements, would be held on backing store in a system
description file. The system builder uses this information to configure the
system. Once the system is loaded, this process would terminate and the first
user process commence.

During the construction and testing phases of system development
some of the processes may not be fully operational or even exist. Processes

already built may not be fully tested and trustworthy. In this situation channel and pool monitors can provide an ideal test harness. Remember that each process is only aware of its environment through the auspices of the channels and pools to which it is attached.

If only a single process has been developed, it is possible to test its operation by connecting its incoming channel to a file of test data, and its outgoing channels to test-result files. Provided that the test data conform to those which the process expects to receive from its neighbours, the process will be unaware that this substitution of test files for real processes has taken place.

The system-description file will be designed to include information about completed processes, along with details as to which processes need to be replaced by test files. The system builder will tell the channel and pool monitors whether to use test files or process-generated data; see figure 3.10. In this way, from the very commencement of construction, the system can be loaded on to a comprehensive test harness.

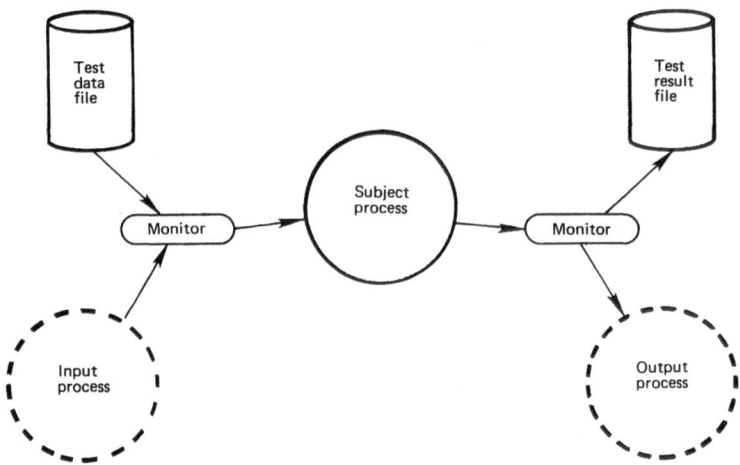

Figure 3.10 Monitor test harness

3.8 EXAMPLE

With the previous discussion in mind, it will be instructive to describe the implementation of a very simple nucleus or 'kernel' of software that will support the real-time machine. We shall make a number of assumptions, as follows.

(1) The system will be implemented using a single CPU. If this is the case, then we can ensure that a process has temporary uninterrupted use of the processor by disabling the interrupt mechanism.

(2) There are no interrupting devices. We shall make this simplifying assumption until we discuss scheduling mechanisms in the next chapter.

(3) There is sufficient main storage in the system to accommodate the code elements of all the processes in the system. Accordingly no memory allocation mechanism or backing store, will be required.

(4) Semaphores will be implemented as the synchronisation primitives.

(5) The kernel resides in a protected area of store. This implies that the kernel can only be entered by means of an interrupt or software trap.

(6) Channels will be implemented as first-in-first-out (FIFO) queues of fixed-sized messages.

To provide the kernel we must facilitate processor sharing, synchronisation and interprocess communication. Before proceeding we will define some useful data structures and data-manipulation routines.

3.8.1 Basic Procedures

We will base the structure of the kernel on queues, and therefore some queue-manipulation routines will be helpful. Every queue will have a HEAD pointer and a TAIL pointer, pointing to the first and the last queue element, respectively. We shall also maintain a SIZE data item for each queue, containing the number of items currently in the queue. Each queue element will include a NEXT pointer, pointing to the next item in the queue. A pointer that points nowhere is NULL.

To remove the first element from a queue and leave it pointed to by a pointer ELEMENT we have

> *Remove ELEMENT from QUEUE*
> (1) Make the value of ELEMENT equal the value of the HEAD pointer of QUEUE
> (2) Make the value of the HEAD of QUEUE equal to the value of NEXT in the item pointed to by HEAD of QUEUE
> (3) Decrement the SIZE of QUEUE.

To insert the element pointed to by ELEMENT into QUEUE we have

> *Insert ELEMENT into QUEUE*
> (1) If the value of HEAD of QUEUE is NULL then make the value of HEAD of QUEUE equal to the value of ELEMENT. Otherwise make the value of NEXT in the item pointed to by TAIL of QUEUE equal to the value of ELEMENT
> (2) Make the value of NEXT in the item pointed to ELEMENT equal to NULL
> (3) Make the value of TAIL of QUEUE equal to the value of ELEMENT
> (4) Make the value of ELEMENT equal to NULL
> (5) Increment the SIZE of QUEUE.

Figures 3.11 and 3.12 show the action of these two procedures. In figure 3.13 various kernel data structures are shown. Process descriptors contain the volatile environments of individual processes and a pointer field, NEXT, for use in creating queues of process descriptors. A semaphore consists of a value field, to hold the current value of the semaphore, and pointer fields that will be used to maintain queues of process descriptors. A simple queue item consists of the two pointers necessary for queue identification, together with the size of the queue. Figure 3.14 shows kernel queues. Each process descriptor will refer to an individual process. It will reside on one of the process descriptor queues, dependent on the status of its process. If the process is the running process, the descriptor will be the sole member of the *running* queue. If the process is waiting for use of the processor, the descriptor will be on the *runnable* queue. If the process is blocked, waiting on a semaphore, then the descriptor will be on the queue associated with the semaphore.

To complete our list of basic tools, we still need two procedures to affect process swapping

Save status of PROCESS
Store contents of all registers and other vital status information in the volatile environment area of the process descriptor pointed to by PROCESS.

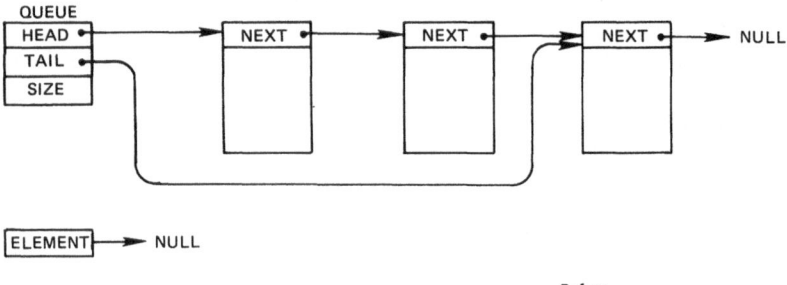

· · · · Before

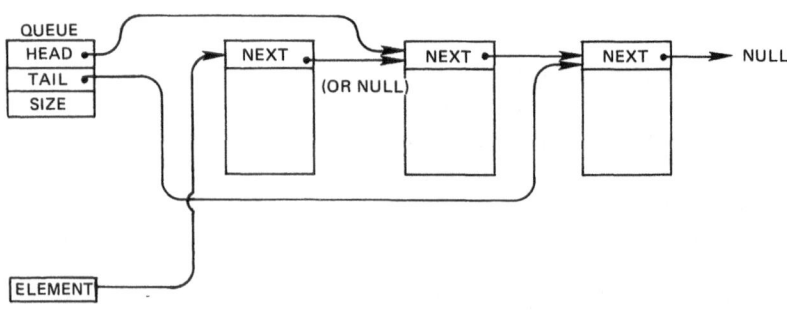

· · · · After

Figure 3.11 Remove ELEMENT from QUEUE

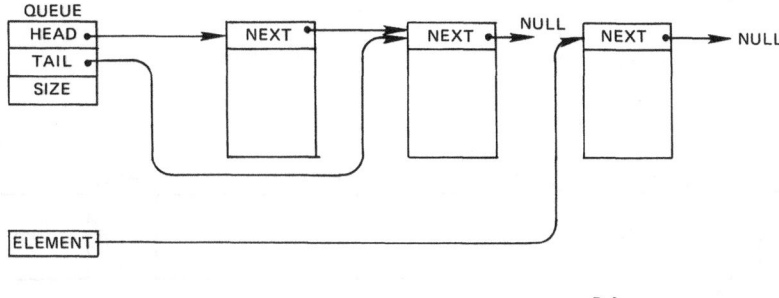

· · · · Before

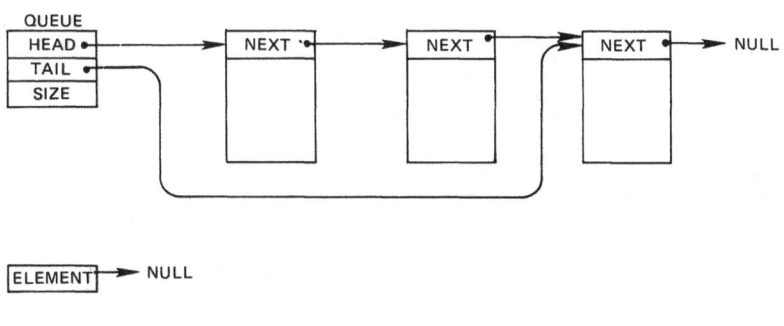

· · · · After

Figure 3.12 Insert ELEMENT into QUEUE

Restore status of PROCESS

Fill registers and status words with information obtained from the
volatile environment area of process descriptor pointed to by **PROCESS**.

3.8.2 Process Sharing and Synchronisation

Now, the running process remains the running process until such time as it is
forced to stop by executing a **WAIT** operation. A **SIGNAL** operation may render

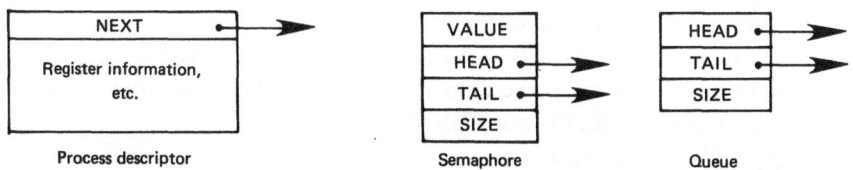

Figure 3.13 Executive (or kernel) data structures

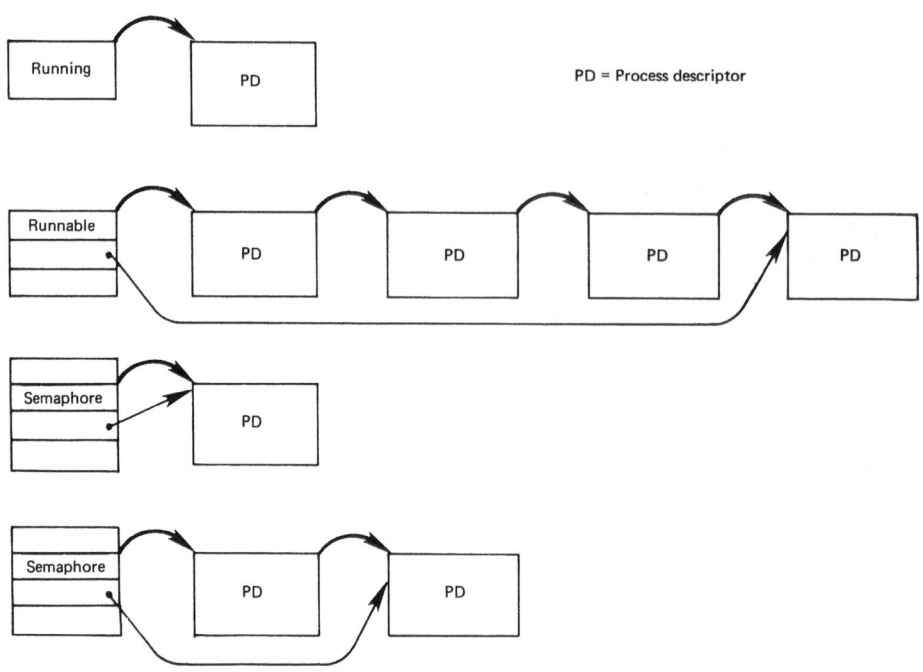

Figure 3.14 Process descriptor queues

runnable a process which is currently blocked. So, assuming that WAIT and SIGNAL are trap handling processes, we define three processes that will implement processor sharing and synchronisation. WAIT on SEM and SIGNAL SEM will implement the two synchronisation primitivies, and the dispatcher will effect the process swapping.

WAIT on SEM
(1) Lock out interrupts
(2) Save status of RUNNING
(3) If the value of the semaphore SEM is not equal to zero then reduce the value by one; otherwise, insert RUNNING into SEM queue
(4) Unlock interrupts
(5) Exit to dispatcher.

SIGNAL SEM
(1) Lock out interrupts
(2) Save status of RUNNING
(3) If the value of HEAD of the SEM queue is NULL then increase the value of SEM by one; otherwise, remove ELEMENT from SEM queue, then insert ELEMENT into RUNNABLE
(4) Unlock interrupts
(5) Exit to dispatcher.

Dispatcher

(1) Lock out interrupts

(2) If the value of RUNNING is NULL then remove RUNNING from RUNNABLE

(3) Restore status of RUNNING

(4) Unlock interrupts.

3.8.3 Communication Facilities

3.8.3.1 Channels

The channels in the system will be based on queues. When needed, elements for the channels will be obtained from the system freespace queue. When no longer required, the elements will be returned to the freespace queue. To avoid corruption of the queue pointers, it will be necessary to protect the queues from simultaneous access by more than one process. For this reason we will provide two semaphores for each queue.

If a piece of code is bracketed by WAIT and SIGNAL on the same semaphore, and the semaphore is given an initial value of one, then only one process at a time may execute the bracketed code. If a semaphore is used in this way, it is called a mutual-exclusion semaphore. The first queue semaphore, then, will have an initial value of one, and be used to ensure that only one process is manipulating the queue at any one time. The second semaphore will have an initial value equal to the number of items in the queue, and be used to ensure that a process accessing items from the queue cannot do so if the queue is empty. The user processes will not have direct access to the queues and semaphores; they will only have the ability to call monitor procedures.

One fundamental queue in the system is the system freespace queue, ·FREESPACE. The semaphore *freespace-not-empty* is initially set to the number of items in the freespace queue, and the *freespace-mutual-exclusion-semaphore* set to one. The freespace monitor will provide the following access procedures:

Get item for QUEUE

(1) WAIT on queue-mutual-exclusion-semaphore

(2) WAIT on freespace-not-empty

(3) WAIT on freespace-mutual-exclusion-semaphore

(4) Remove ELEMENT from FREESPACE then insert ELEMENT into QUEUE

(5) SIGNAL freespace-mutual-exclusion-semaphore

(6) SIGNAL queue-mutual-exclusion-semaphore

Return ELEMENT

(1) WAIT on freespace-mutual-exclusion-semaphore

(2) Insert ELEMENT into FREESPACE

(3) SIGNAL freespace-mutual-exclusion-semaphore

(4) SIGNAL freespace-not-empty

3.8.3.2 Pools

The detailed operation of the pool monitor-access procedures will depend on the structure of the pool data. We can, however, postulate a number of access rules: no process may write to a pool while other processes are reading it; no reader may start to read a pool if it is currently being written to by another process; more than one process may read the pool at one time.

In the following access procedures the purpose of the *mutex* (mutual exclusion) semaphore is to ensure that only one process may manipulate the integer *readcount* at any one time. Similarly, semaphore *w* allows only one process to write to the pool at any given time.

> Initial values:
> Integer readcount = 0
> Semaphores mutex, *w* =1.

> *Read pool*
> code A: WAIT on mutex
> readcount = readcount + 1
> if readcount equals 1 then WAIT on *w*
> SIGNAL mutex
> .
> .
> Do Reading
> .
> .
>
> code B: WAIT on *w*
> readcount = readcount − 1
> if readcount equals 0 then SIGNAL *w*
> SIGNAL mutex .

> *Write pool*
> WAIT on *w*
> .
> .
> Do Writing
> .
> .
> SIGNAL *w*

Assume now that a process wishes to read, and that the value of *mutex* is one. The process executes a WAIT operation on *mutex*, decrements the semaphore and passes on. It sets *readcount* to one and, accordingly, executes the WAIT on *w* operation. Note that while this process is in this section of code, no other reader may enter since *mutex* is currently equal to zero. The reader will only pass the WAIT on *w* operation when *w* has the value unity. Therefore if a writer is currently writing it will have decremented w, and so the reader cannot continue until the writer executes the SIGNAL w operation, at the completion of writing. The reader then passes into the reading code, having decremented w (ensuring no writing) and incremented *mutex*. More readers can now, one by one, enter code A. As *readcount* will now be greater than one, they will not WAIT on w and more than one process can be reading. Code B decrements the readcount and, when there are no more readers in the reading code, signals w, allowing a reader into the reading code, or a writer into the writing code, but not both. Notice that this arrangement could cause a writer to wait indefinitely while readers read.

Thus we complete the basic kernel of a real-time machine. We shall return to this discussion at the end of the next chapter.

3.9 SUMMARY

We have described the software that would be necessary to support the existence of processes, channels and pools. It is necessary to provide, possibly by sharing the resources, a CPU, memory and executable code for every process in the system. To control the access to channels and pools we must provide WAIT and SIGNAL operations and access-monitor routines. These facilities are centred in the executive or kernel. We have detailed the 'special' executive processes that make up the kernel of software necessary to support our virtual real-time machine. We must now provide a scheduling mechanism.

Concepts

Multiplexing; multiprogramming; volatile environment; swapping; process descriptor; serially re-usable; re-entrant; queue; hopper; monitor; executive; protection; memory management

4 Scheduling

The next facility to be discussed is the scheduling of process activity. The design of the virtual machine enables the software designer to separate considerations of process scheduling from those of process design. The processes think that they have sole use of their own processor and memory. In a one-process-per processor setup, the processes can be thought of as running continuously, subject only to synchronisation requirements; in this case the scheduling problem does not arise. However, in a multiprocessing environment, the allocation of CPU/memory to the processes must be organised by agencies within the system. As a total concept, scheduling consists of deciding *when* the CPU/memory will be re-scheduled; *how* the CPU/memory will be re-scheduled; and *which* new process will be chosen. When and how to re-schedule have been discussed in the previous chapter. Here we will discuss how the system selects suitable candidate processes when a CPU/memory comes up for re-allocation — the *which*.

Priority

Selecting a process to be run is a function of the relative importance of all eligible processes. Obviously the process selected should be that which is most important or vital for the system's operation. The scheduling problem involves deciding which is the 'most important process'. It is convenient to think of process importance in terms of priority — a more important process having a higher priority than a less important one.

Priorities are not necessarily fixed. Conceptually, a process that samples a fluid flow rate every 5 minutes should gain in priority as the 5-minute period is approached. The more flexible the allocation of priorities in a system, the more flexible will be the system's response to changing environmental conditions.

Response

Most commercial computer operating systems attempt to maximise the use of computing resources (disc drives, tape units, etc.). Accordingly, the priority of a certain process at a particular time may be strongly influenced by what resources it will use. Clearly, it is desirable to run a process that uses a tape unit at a time when the tape unit would otherwise be idle. However, once the system is expected to operate in real-time, the prime consideration must become that of adequate response to its environment. What is regarded as an adequate response will depend on the application. Real-time considerations must take precedence over the economic use of system resources. Our primary aim must be to design a solution to the scheduling problem that will ensure an adequate real-time response from the system.

Real-time Priority Levels

A process's priority is dependent on how important it is for the process to run immediately upon the occurrence of a particular event. This event may be something occurring in the controlled system, or simply the passing of a certain amount of time. The more stringent the deadline the process has to meet, the higher its priority.

Three broad levels of priority can be identified

(1) An interrupt level, which holds the service routines for those devices and situations that require instant or near-instant service;
(2) a synchronous, or clock level, on which repetitive processes such as scanning and sampling are run; these processes require accurate timing for their activation;
(3) the lowest or base level, which includes the processes that do not have to meet deadlines.

Pre-emptive and Non-pre-emptive Strategies

In order that the currently running processes reflect the relative process priorities in effect at a particular time, we shall specify a pre-emptive scheduling strategy. By this we mean that, if a process wishes to be activated, and it has a higher priority than the process currently running, then the current process will be stopped so that the high-priority process may proceed. For example, if a base level process is running , and a device interrupts, the relevant interrupt level service process does not wait for the base level process to finish, but will be executed immediately, before the base level process is resumed.

The alternative, a non-pre-emptive approach, would imply that the processes, be they interrupt, clock or base level, run to completion without interruption. Upon completion, each process would transfer control to the dispatching mechanism.

Significant advantages are obtained when using this latter technique. Since the processes are not interruptable, poor synchronisation does not give rise to the problem of corruption of shared data. Shared subroutines can be implemented without producing re-entrant code or implementing lock and unlock mechanisms. However, as we have indicated in chapter 3, the main drawback with this approach is that while the current process is running the system is not responsive to changes in the environment. Therefore, system processes must be extremely brief if the real-time response system is not to be impaired. So, for the purpose of the following discussion we shall assume a pre-emptive strategy.

4.1   INTERRUPT LEVEL

It is at this level of process that the neat division between *when* to re-schedule and *which* to re-schedule becomes somewhat blurred. An interrupt forces a re-scheduling of the CPU to the corresponding interrupt-handling process. The system has no control over the timing of this re-scheduling. For this reason the amount of processing carried out at this level must be kept to a minimum. Normally, an interrupt level process will only do sufficient processing to avoid loss of data and status information and will then channel the resulting information to a lower priority process for further servicing.

The interrupt forces a re-scheduling, and therefore the interrupt level processes must conduct a form of process swapping. As discussed in chapter 3, the hardware assists in the initial stages. The interrupt processes are designed to store whatever parts of the interrupted process's volatile environment they may need to use (normally a number of registers). They then carry out the necessary processing, replace the volatile environment and exit.

Even within the interrupt level, a priority structure will be necessary. The priority levels within the interrupt processes are defined by the relative time-critical nature of the interrupting devices. High-speed devices — for example, disc units — will need the ability to pre-empt the interrupt level processes associated with a slower device. The priority scheduling will normally be imposed by the hardware priority interrupt mechanism available on most modern processors. In general, these mechanisms work as follows.

The hardware includes a number of interrupt lines, each associated with an interrupt priority level. The CPU includes a register in which the current priority is stored (the processor priority). Associated with each interrupt line is a pair of memory locations (interrupt vector). The first of these locations holds the address of the start of the interrupt handling process for that interrupt line/priority level. When a device wishes to interrupt, it puts a signal on an interrupt line. If the processor priority is currently greater than the priority of the interrupted line, the interrupt is ignored. If not, then the current program counter is stored in the second location of the interrupt vector, the processor priority becomes that of the interrupting line and the value in the first location of the interrupt vector is placed in the program counter. When the interrupt handling process completes, it lowers the processor priority and replaces the program counter with the value previously stored in the second location of the interrupt vector. Note that interrupt handling processes may be interrupted by higher-priority interrupts.

4.2 CLOCK LEVEL

4.2.1 The Real-time Clock

One of the interrupt-level processes is the real-time clock handler. A real-time clock is a hardware device which interrupts the processor at a regular rate. Virtually all real-time systems include such a device. The reason for its inclusion is threefold.

First, not all activities carried out by a real-time system are a response to some external stimulus or interrupt. Very often, physical constraints (lack of available interrupt lines, for example) will prevent the device or mechanism that is being controlled from interrupting the processor. Therefore, in order to ascertain the need for servicing, it becomes necessary for the real-time system to inspect the status of the device at regular intervals. This technique, called polling, is used widely in communications systems to control distant terminals. The interval between servicing will, of course, be dependent on the performance characteristics of the device. Ideally, system control should be centred on the CPU. Interrupting devices command the attention of the CPU and are therefore exercising a degree of control. By regularly scanning the status of the devices, the CPU avoids the need for interrupt and retains full control of the system. It is necessary, then, for the system to be aware of the passing of real time so that it may activate device-servicing routines at relevant times.

Second, many devices controlled by the system will operate extremely slowly when compared with the speed of the CPU. This is especially true of electromechanical devices such as motors and relays. A process that causes a relay to close cannot assume that a relay has in fact closed immediately after execution of the instructions that initiate closure.

The process may well have to wait 20 to 50 ms before the relay is sure to be closed. It will, therefore, be necessary for the process to be able to wait a certain known amount of actual time before continuing.

Third, it will often be necessary for the system to have a knowledge of real clock time in terms of a 24-hour day. In this way exact timing of certain events can be noted, stored and recalled for later report and statistics production.

The real-time clock interrupting at regular intervals provides the system with a knowledge of, and thus the ability to measure, the passing of time. The rate at which a clock interrupts will depend upon the timing accuracy required by the system. It will usually be defined by the required rate of activation of the most often activated device-servicing routine. Typical values would be 20, 50 or 100 ms.

4.2.2 Clock Level Processes

Clock priority level processes are those which must run at strictly regular intervals. The real-time clock interrupt handling process, when activated, will normally update the time-of-day counter (some memory location) and transfer control to the dispatcher, having first left an indication that a real-time clock interrupt has just occurred. It is then up to the dispatching mechanism to select any clock level processes that must run at that clock 'tick'.

　　　Some of the clock level processes will require accurate timing for their activation (the very reason they are at clock level). If the processes requiring the most accurate timing are always run first after a real-time clock interrupt, then they will be initiated at a regular rate. Those scheduled later will have some 'jitter' caused by the varying running times of the previously run processes. Here, priority is decided by the process's sensitivity to variations in timing.

　　　It is possible, in certain circumstances, for processes running at clock level to take longer than the period between clock interrupts. Rather than let these momentary overloads disrupt the other processes that require high timing accuracy, it is possible to split the processes into two priority classes. The high-priority processes that are guaranteed to finish within the clock interrupt period are run first. Thereafter, the lower-priority clock level processes run the risk of being interrupted by the real-time clock on its next 'tick'.

　　　The real-time clock will be designed to interrupt sufficiently often to initiate those clock level processes requiring the most frequent activation. Obviously, not all of the clock level processes will need to run at that rate; some will require activation every 5 clock 'ticks', some every 50 perhaps. A widely used method for scheduling these processes is to use a 'bit map' technique. This is explained in the following discussion and illustrated in figure 4.1.

　　　Each clock tick is numbered, modulo N, where N is the number of ticks that will result in the eventual activation of all processes. This tick number is used as an index to a timetable, each word of which has various bits set to indicate the different processes to be run at that tick. If a **WAIT** synchronising operation has been executed, a clock-level process may not be runnable for some time. If this is the case, then the relevant bit in the activation mask will not be set. The tick number selects the word within the bit map. This word is logically 'anded' with the activation mask. The resultant word is then scanned from the most significant bit and the processes whose bits are set are executed in sequence. Note that the priorities of these processes are defined by the position of the process's column within the map.

4.2.3 The Clock Queue

In the clock priority level we include device-scanning and polling processes that have stringent timing requirements. There is, however, another class of processes that use the real-time clock interrupt. These processes wish to 'delay' their

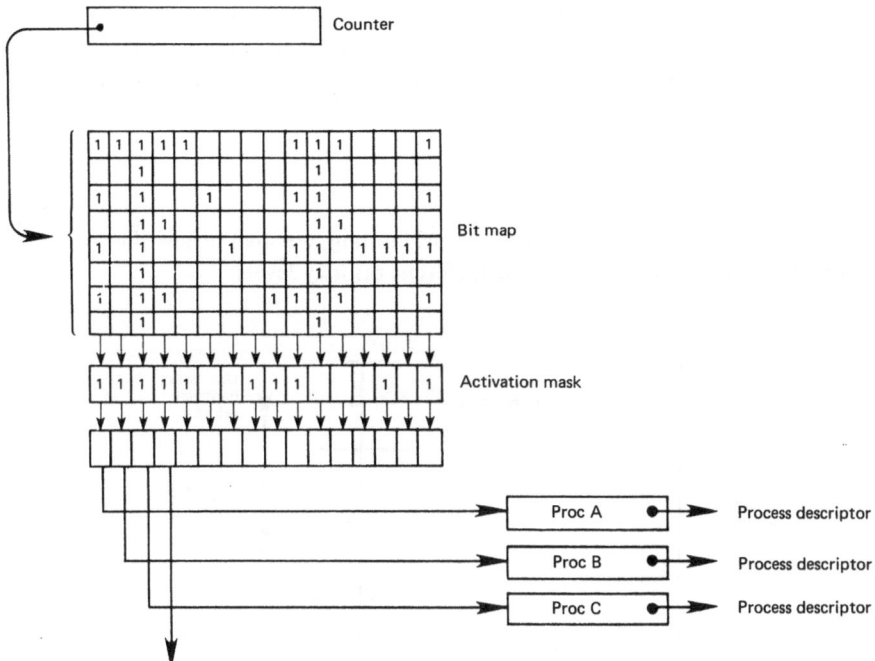

Figure 4.1 Bit map

activities for a fixed amount of time. The process cited earlier, which closed
a relay, is such an example. We will set the priority of these processes within
the base level group. Should it be vital that a process run immediately upon the
expiry of its delay period, then we could allocate to it the highest-level base
priority.

A common method of implementing this delay capability is to introduce
a 'clock queue' of process descriptors. When a process wishes to be delayed for
a certain length of time, it calls upon an executive subroutine to remove its
process descriptor from the runnable list and place it on the clock queue. The
clock queue is a list of process descriptors of processes that have requested
suspension. The process descriptor is placed in the list in a position relative to
the time at which re-activation is required. When the real-time clock interrupts,
the interrupt handling process updates the time-of-day counter. It then checks
to see if this time corresponds to the time of the re-activation of the first
process(es) in the clock list. If so, the process is made runnable by transferring
the process descriptor to the queue of runnable processes.

This repetitive checking of the clock list may be considered an unacceptable
overhead for the real-time clock handler. After all, the interrupt handlers are
meant to be short! To reduce this overhead, a special clock level process
can be constructed. This process, designed to be activated every so many
clock ticks, does the checking and process descriptor swapping. The period

between successive activations of this process will define the minimum integral delay interval possible in the system. For example, if the process is activated every 20 ms, other processes may only delay themselves by 20, 40, 60 ms etc.

4.2.4 A Review

Before proceeding to discuss base level scheduling, we shall review the situation to date. Figure 4.2 summarises the different priority levels.

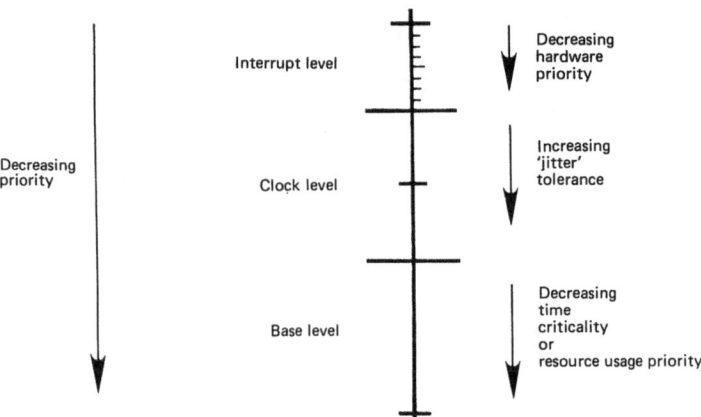

Figure 4.2 Priority levels

Figure 4.3 shows a graph of process priority level against time. In this idealised diagram, it is assumed that each process has a unique priority and that the dispatcher takes zero time to do its job. The diagram represents the following sequence. Initially, a base level process is running, when a clock interrupt occurs. The clock interrupt handling process takes over and carries out any necessary processing before handing over to the highest-priority clock level process that is currently runnable. When this process finishes, a lower-priority clock level process takes over until it, in its turn, completes. The highest-priority base level process is then allocated the processor until it temporarily loses use of the processor to an interrupt handling process. In due course, the next clock interrupt occurs and the cycle is repeated.

4.3   BASE LEVEL

Once the processing requirements of clock level processes have been met, the remaining time in a clock period is available for use by the base level processes. Various scheduling methods can be applied at this level.

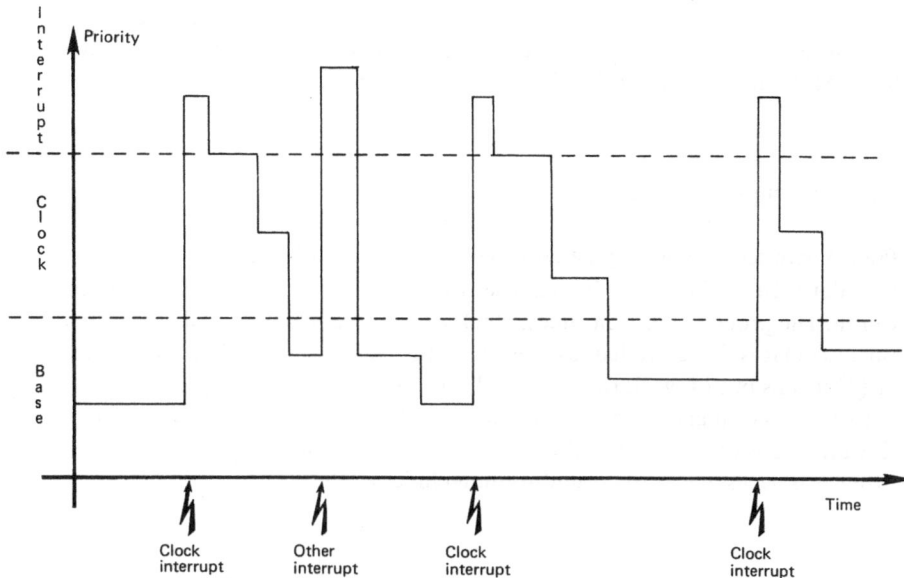

Figure 4.3 Priority vs time

4.3.1 Time Slicing on a Round-robin Basis

This is relatively straightforward. At each clock period, one of the base level processes is selected to be run for the remainder of the period. This selection is done on a round-robin basis, a new process being selected each period. If the selected process, when activated, has no work to carry out, it returns control to the dispatcher immediately after it is activated. The dispatcher then chooses the next in line. Similarly, if the chosen process terminates before the end of the clock period, it returns control to the dispatcher.

Of course this method takes no account of the relative priorities of the base level processes. An implicit priority scheme can be introduced by giving higher-priority processes extra clock periods when their turn comes round on the round-robin. An alternative method is to set up a round-robin where higher-priority processes have more than one place on the round-robin, and are therefore selected more often. Re-scheduling the processes every clock period may prove too high an overhead, and so the dispatcher may re-schedule after every so many clock ticks.

In order to implement the round-robin method it is only necessary to provide the dispatcher with a circular list of runnable processes, and include within the dispatcher sufficient intelligence to maintain the round-robin.

If we follow the basic philosophy that systems should always be as simple as possible, then the round-robin method provides the most applicable strategy.

In many situations, a simple policy such as this will suffice. The designer should introduce more complex methods only when simple methods have been shown (by measurement of system performance) to be inadequate.

4.3.2 Pre-emptive Policies

Pre-emptive scheduling may be regarded as a variation on the round-robin technique. Here, the dispatcher chooses the highest-priority base level process to run. The process then continues, clock period after clock period, until such time as (1) it is forced to halt as a result of the execution of a **WAIT** operation, or (2) it runs out of work to do and voluntarily relinquishes the processor, or (3) a process of higher priority becomes eligible for selection. An advantage of this method is that the dispatcher is not directed to swap the processes as often as is necessary in the round-robin technique.

4.3.3 Priority Allocation among Base Level Processes

The priority assigned to a process may be fixed for the life of the system, or it may vary, dependent upon the conditions affecting the system at a particular time.

Fixed Priority

Process priority can be fixed and assigned at the time the process is created. Its priority would then be a function of the urgency of the job it must perform and often of the 'cost' or availability of the system resources that it uses.

Unfortunately, it is very difficult for a designer accurately to forecast what will be a satisfactory mix of priorities for base level processes. This problem is aggravated by the dynamic and unpredictable nature of the system's environment. We can gain useful knowledge and experience by examining similar systems, but if this previous experience is not available then other methods must be used to gain information on system behaviour. This can be done either by analysing simulation models of the system, or by monitoring actual system behaviour under different priority mixes and environmental conditions. Chapter 8 will discuss this activity.

Variable Priority – The High-level Scheduler

The problem of forecasting can be avoided if process priorities are varied dynamically, dependent on the behaviour of the system when it is in operation. The *high-level scheduler* can be pressed into service to fulfil this function.

This is an executive process that has the ability to alter process priority. It is activated at regular intervals and uses its knowledge of over-all system status to re-allocate process priority. The calculation of new process priorities is an overhead on the system's workload, and so the algorithm that it uses should be as simple as possible. An example of a useful algorithm would be to give a higher priority than normal to a process whose input channel was growing excessively large. For commercial, batch-based operating systems, the algorithm chosen would be one that would tend to maximise the use of system resources or throughput of user jobs. For a real-time system, however, the algorithm must ensure that the time-critical processes are carried out. Therefore, when allocating a priority to one process, it must take into consideration process deadlines. More complex priority allocation algorithms will take into consideration the deadlines of *all* the processes in the system.

System Overload

The scheduling algorithm for a real-time system must also ensure that the system adjusts itself to an overload situation in a correct manner. As an example, take a message switching system that receives and stores messages. Once a message is received in its entirety by the message switch, it is then re-transmitted down a selected path. Ideally, the message switch should never refuse incoming messages. Therefore, in an overload situation, the process reading in and storing messages must gain a high priority compared with the path selection and transmitting processes. This dynamic adjustment to overload is a necessity in all real-time systems and may, in cases of heavy overload, involve the system in temporary abandonment of some of its less vital activities. It is necessary for the designer to know what is the desired, acceptable or tolerable behaviour of the system under overload conditions. The formulation of suitable dynamic priority allocation algorithms is his most powerful tool in implementing these overload characteristics.

4.4   RESOURCE SHARING AND DEADLOCK

All processes in the system use system resources. At the least, these resources consist of a processor and storage for the code element. More usually, the resources would include disc files and peripheral devices. Whenever two or more processes compete for the use of a set of resources, a possibility of deadlock exists. Imagine that process A has the exclusive use of resource R and requests use of resource Q. Process B has the exclusive use of resource Q but requests use of R. Neither process can continue — they are deadlocked.

Commercial operating systems apply one of three strategies to solve the deadlock problem

(1) prevent deadlock by ensuring that the conditions necessary for deadlock cannot occur;

(2) detect deadlock when it occurs and instigate recovery action;

(3) anticipate that deadlock may occur and try to avoid the situation that will cause it.

The simplest strategy is to demand that any process be allocated all of its resources at one time (normally when it starts). This approach avoids the possible deadlock, but it does not allow for the optimum use of system resources. Complex deadlock-avoidance algorithms have been designed and applied, in an attempt to allow more efficient sharing of resources between the competing processes. However, in a real-time system, the processing time required for the more sophisticated algorithms may prove unacceptable.

If we chose the simplest strategy, as described above, then the ideal process for allocating the resources is the high-level scheduler. The configuration and status of resources in the system would be described in system data structures. Each of these data structures (pools) would be protected by its monitor. The scheduler would carry out its resource allocation task via a dialogue with the resource monitors. In a real-time system, the resource-allocation responsibilities of the scheduler would focus on avoiding deadlock situations. Obviously, time limits permitting, it would be helpful if the scheduler could also cater for the optimum usage of system resources.

Figure 4.4 shows a possible layout for the processes involved in scheduling. The dispatcher would be a simple process primarily concerned with swapping the volatile environment of the process that is indicated in the process descriptor

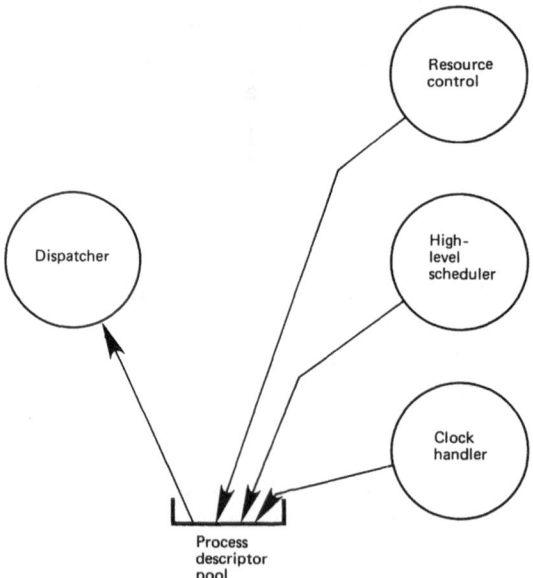

Figure 4.4 Scheduling processes

pool as the next to be run. The other three processes would use their particular knowledge of system status to manipulate the process descriptors so that they reflect the current priority requirements.

4.5 EXAMPLE

The scheduling strategy implied by the very simple kernel described in section 3.8 is simply: 'each process continues execution until it loses use of the CPU by executing an unsuccessful WAIT operation.' For the sake of simplicity we did not include any interrupting devices in the system. Now, we will make the example more realistic by adding the following two assumptions.

(1) The system hardware includes a real-time clock.
(2) The CPU is provided with a priority vectored interrupt mechanism.

With these two facilities we can implement a more sophisticated scheduling arrangement. The scheduling of interrupt level processes is taken care of by the interrupt handling hardware. By using the real-time clock and its handling process, we can very easily produce a simple round-robin scheduling mechanism for the remaining processes. Consider the following processes.

Clock Interrupt Handler
(1) Save status of RUNNING
(2) Update time-of-day counter
(3) Set flag indicating clock interrupt
(4) Exit to dispatcher.

Dispatcher
(1) Lock out interrupts
(2) If clock interrupt flag set then insert RUNNING into RUNNABLE and remove RUNNING from RUNNABLE
(3) Restore status of RUNNING
(4) Reset clock interrupt flag
(5) Unlock interrupts.

We now have a simple time-slicing round-robin. But the system still has no concept of priority for non interrupt level processes. In order to make scheduling more sensitive to process priority, we must extend our simple process descriptor to indicate the process's priority. We do this by introducing a new element into the process descriptor data structure. This element holds a value that reflects the priority of the process. We must be able to assume that the process descriptors in the RUNNABLE, and possibly the semaphore queues, are always in priority order. To do this we must extend our 'insert into queue' procedure so that it places the process descriptors at the correct location in the queues.

Introduction to Real-time Software Design

4.6 SUMMARY

We have added a process-scheduling facility to our virtual machine. Scheduling
is based on process priority. We have identified three levels of priority —
interrupt, clock and base level. Because of the time-critical nature of the system,
we have emphasised a time-deadline policy, rather than a policy that would
optimise resource utilisation. The design of scheduling strategies is totally
divorced from the design of the scheduled processes. The scheduling mechanisms
used are standard models of processes, channels and pools. The framework
of our virtual real-time machine is complete. A further problem remains, that
of attempting to ensure system reliability.

Concepts

Priority; clock; bit map; time slicing; round-robin; pre-emption; high-level
scheduler; deadlock; system resources

5 Reliability

Real-time systems must be reliable. Ideally they will perform in a fault-free manner throughout their lifetime. In reality, this is rarely the case: systems *will* fail from time to time. Hardware systems fail when their components wear out, but software cannot 'wear out'. Why then does a software system fail?

Software Faults

First of all, faults appear in software when particular circumstances occur which have not been catered for in the original design or, alternatively, when an error has been made at the coding stage and is not revealed during testing. As a result, the software does not perform in the correct manner. It can be stated with certainty that all software harbours a number of undetected design and implementation errors. It would therefore be unrealistic to assume that any piece of software is perfect, but one can demand that it perform to an acceptable level of reliability. What is deemed to be 'acceptable' will depend on the application concerned. Obviously the impact of a breakdown will have more serious implications for some systems than others.

System Availability

Reliability requirements are often expressed in terms of system availability: a system will be expected to perform with a certain maximum allowable time out of service during a particular time period. Also, no breakdown should take the system out of service for more than a specified time.

Using a hardware engineering analogy, reliability requirements are expressed in terms of *mean time to repair* (MTTR) and *mean time between failure* (MTBF). Two factors, then, are important for system availability: (1) how rapidly the fault can be repaired; and (2) how often the system fails.

Consider the first point. Before the fault can be repaired, the cause must be isolated. Unless the software is well structured, and well documented, this can be a lengthy and tedious activity. Well-structured software increases system availability because it is easier to maintain. Further, if system availability is to be increased, the software must be designed to provide maintenance personnel with as much diagnostic information as possible in the event of failure.

The second point implies that system failures should be kept to a minimum in the first place. This chapter will concern itself with the methods of reducing the frequency of these failures.

5.1   TESTING

Software faults can be attributed to residual design and coding errors or omissions. Reliability, then, is strongly influenced by the success of the testing phase of product development. Testing can only indicate the presence of errors, not their absence. To ensure maximum reliability, testing should expose the largest possible proportion of errors in the product. It is impossible to remove all the errors in a piece of software of any complexity. It should, however, be possible to gain a quantitative measure of the effectiveness of testing and, from this, to extrapolate a measure of future reliability.

The occurrence of a software failure implies that a fault has been exposed by the execution of some untested pathway in the code. In the case of real-time software, further faults arise as a result of the occurrence of untested timing conditions. Ideally, testing should thoroughly exercise the software and thus expose all faults. Unfortunately this is impossible. Even if we leave aside the problem of timing errors, it remains impractical, for all but the simplest module, to test every pathway through the code. Take the simple module modelled by the flow graph shown in figure 5.1. There are approximately 250 thousand million unique pathways through this module. Even if we could test one path every millisecond it would take eight years to test the module exhaustively. Clearly it is impossible completely to test large programs, but there are a number of tools and techniques available to increase the effectiveness of the testing that *is* done.

Structured Walkthroughs

One of the most successful software engineering techniques is the structured walkthrough. Here, a small group of people associated with a particular module — the designer, the implementer, the tester — meet together to read through the module code, highlighting the errors and any inconsistencies for later correction. This concentrated code scrutiny has proven to be a potent tool for uncovering errors. However it can be time-consuming and hence expensive.

Profilers

Once the code is submitted for testing, it is necessary to have some quantitative

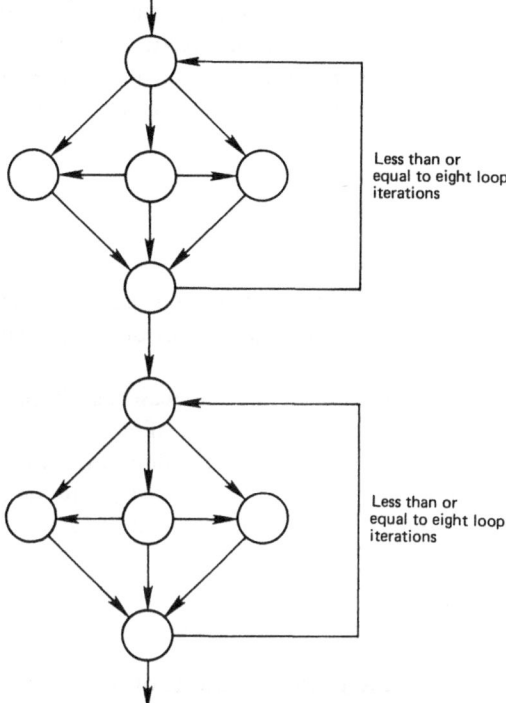

Less than or
equal to eight loop
iterations

Less than or
equal to eight loop
iterations

Figure 5.1 Program flow graph

gauge of the thoroughness of the testing. We know it cannot be done completely. Even if it is not possible to test every pathway through the code, it should be possible to test every branch in the program. During a test run, profiling programs (see section 8.3.2) can be used to generate a source listing of the tested programs with an indication as to which branches have been executed and which not. This information gives the designer an indication of how thorough the test has been, and where further testing should be directed.

Test-data Generators

A more comprehensive tool is a test-data generation system. This tool analyses the structure of the program and produces a control flow graph. Using this graph, and working either from the beginning or the end of the program, the tool traverses the graph, generating a set of input data that will cause all, or a specific sub-set, of the branches to be executed.

5.1.1 Testing and Reliability

Unfortunately, even if all these techniques and tools are used it remains impossible to guarantee that a program is free of faults. The number and seriousness of the residual faults bear a close relationship to the future reliability of the program. It is therefore vital for the designer to have some idea of the number of faults remaining in the software in order to gauge future reliability.

Error Models

The history of a module under test can provide insight into its future reliability. At the commencement of testing, a large number of the more obvious errors will be uncovered.

Later, the rate of fault exposure will decrease, as any remaining errors are necessarily more obscure. From the history of error detection it may be possible to create a mathematical model of the rate of occurrence of errors. Using this model it may further be possible to extrapolate the error rate into the future and thus to obtain a measure of future module reliability.

Error Seeding

Some practitioners attempt to gauge the success of testing by adding known errors to the module. The location and nature of these errors is unknown to the test team; however, they are assumed to have a similar distribution of location and nature as the 'real' errors in the software. After a period of testing, the percentage of 'seeded' errors that have been uncovered is calculated. The figure is assumed to be the same as the percentage of 'real' errors detected. From this information, the number of real errors remaining in the module can be calculated. Needless to say, the seeded errors are removed at the end of the exercise.

5.2   FAULT TOLERANCE

A more positive approach to reliability is to design the system in such a way that the system itself can recover from faults. If this is possible then the system will demand human intervention only when its automatic recovery mechanism cannot cope with the failure. By designing the system to automatically recover from error, we drastically increase the system availability.

Systems that can continue operation in spite of faults are referred to as fault-tolerant systems. If a system is tolerant of faults, it implies that the system can detect the fault when it occurs, have sufficient information about the fault to correct its impact on the system as a whole and can then continue correct operation. Most software systems carry out the fault correction by means of 'rolling back'. Upon the detection of an error the system is returned to a state that existed prior to the fault, and then restarted. The system is restarted from a point called a *checkpoint*, where the system is known to have been operating correctly. We shall discuss this technique in more detail in section 5.4.1. Of course, if the fault is due to an error in the software then the system will fail again if the same conditions are encountered.

Note, in passing, that a great deal of work has been carried out to ensure the reliability of hardware systems. The conventional approach is to use some form of protective redundancy scheme. Here the continued operation of the functions of a particular module is assured by the inclusion of one or more identical, but redundant, modules in the system. If an error is detected in the running module, a spare module is automatically switched into operation and replaces the faulty one.

A protective redundancy scheme can be very expensive and, since most modern computer hardware has a high mean time between failure, this technique would only be used in systems demanding a very high level of reliability. For the purpose of this discussion, we shall assume that any hardware fault protection mechanisms act autonomously and only inform the software of a malfunction if they are unable to correct the fault themselves.

5.3 FAULT DETECTION

Computer hardware is organised, to a greater or lesser extent, to recognise errors within the hardware system. Parity bits within words or bytes of storage, and majority logic circuits within processing hardware are designed to detect malfunctions. If the hardware is not equipped to handle the error itself, it will normally cause an interrupt to the software.

Errors in the software itself are more difficult to detect; nevertheless, their presence can be uncovered by placing checks at various levels in the software structure. At this stage we shall simply assume that the presence of a fault is signalled to a 'recovery monitor' whose action on receipt of a signal will be discussed later. We will now describe the levels at which fault checks can be included in the software system.

5.3.1 Machine Instruction Level

The system hardware can be used to detect errors introduced by the execution of an individual instruction. Attempts to violate memory protection schemes, to execute privileged instructions or simply to divide by zero can all be detected by the hardware and signalled to the recovery monitor by means of an interrupt.

When part of a process's code element is loaded into the main storage the first thing it can do is ensure that the loading operation has been carried out correctly. For this, a simple checksum technique will suffice. A checksum is a numerical value which is a function of the binary patterns comprising the code of a program. The simplest example would be the value produced by adding together all the words of the program as if they were integer binary numbers.

A checksum is positioned at a known location within the code element. Each time loading occurs, the process can calculate a checksum of the code element. This value is compared with the checksum embedded in the code. A discrepancy causes a fault to be signalled.

5.3.2 Code Module Level

Checks can be included in an attempt to guarantee the correct operation of code modules within the processes. One technique is the use of a *baton.* Here, each module of code passes a unique numerical value to the next module to be executed. This value is the baton. The receiving module checks the value. If it is incorrect, or not the value expected, it would imply that the normal progression from module to module has been upset. A fault would then be signalled.

Assertions

Fault checks can be inserted explicitly to form part of the code itself. This is most conveniently done by including an assertion facility in the program development system. The programmer can embed logical assertions in the code. These normally take the form of statements concerning the expected behaviour of the module at different points in its execution. Should an assertion prove false at run time, a fault is flagged and recovery action taken. The introduction of assertions automatically introduces additional, redundant code into the software.

Assertions take a number of different forms. Range checks ensure that the values of data variables lie within a specified range during execution. State checks verify that certain conditions hold among the program variables. Reasonableness checks analyse data input to or output from a module in an attempt to discover impossible or unlikely values. Figure 5.2 shows the assertion mechanisms available in a typical assertion system. The figure shows an ASSERT

ASSERT $(X(I) \neq X(J))$ FOR ALL (I, J) (1:8) WHERE $(I \neq J)$

This statement asserts the fact that:

For all values of I and J such that $1 \leqslant I, J \leqslant 8$ and $I \neq J$
then $X(I) \neq X(J)$

In other words, at the point in the program code where the assertion is made, all the first eight elements of array X will have unequal values. If this is not the case, the assertion will fail.

Figure 5.2 An assertion statement in the PET system

statement in the Program Evaluation and Test (PET) system produced by the Macdonell Douglas Corporation (Stuki, 1978).

In a real-time software environment, assertion mechanisms are of most value during the construction and testing phase. The existence of assertion mechanisms, however, implies extra code, which can produce an unacceptable overhead in a running system. Therefore the provision of assertion code can be made optional at the compilation stage. During the testing phase, the module could be compiled including all the assertions in the program code. Later, the module could be recompiled including only a subset of the original assertions, the remainder being translated as program comments. Ideally, as many assertions as possible should be left in the code, since they are a powerful tool for detecting errors at the code module level.

5.3.3 Process Level

Channel and pool monitors provide an ideal error detection mechanism. Because they form the external interface between processes and provide processes with their interaction with the 'outside world', they can be used to watch for unexpected, and therefore possibly incorrect, process behaviour.

Any data being transferred out of the process can be checked and an error flagged if it appears suspicious. A monitor could be set up to initiate a time counter for each of the processes feeding its channel or pool. Should any of the processes not provide output within a certain time period, then an error condition can be flagged. Similarly, the fact that a channel begins to overfill could well indicate a fault in the receiving process. The monitor may not be able to pinpoint the exact cause of an error, but it will be able to indicate that certain processes are acting in a suspicious manner.

These fault checks will impose an overhead on the performance of the monitor. It would be desirable to make error-checking code an optional facility. This is commonly done in two ways. First, at compile time, successively detailed levels of error-checking code can be included in the monitor by conditional compilation facilities. Secondly, at run time, a pool of on/off switch data items could be set up. A monitor would regularly check the status of one or more of these switches and, dependent on this information, execute levels of error-checking code. A process associated with the system operator's console would change the value of the data switches when commanded by the operator.

5.3.4 Audit Level

Whole processes can be introduced into the system with the sole purpose of error detection. These 'audit' processes continually check system pools and hardware status for invalid status or conditions. They flag an error if their in-built view of 'correct' operation detects any discrepancies.

Watchdogs

A specialised type of auditor is the watchdog timer process. Figure 5.3 illustrates a watchdog set-up. The watchdog process, W, operating at clock level, regularly decrements the value of a set of data items in the pool. Each data item relates to one of the set of subject processes $S_1, \ldots, S_n$. The subject processes are designed to reset their data items at particular points in their execution cycle. Now, should a watchdog process, on decrementing all the data items, discover that one of the items has gone below a certain value (usually zero), it signals an error indicating the relevant subject process.

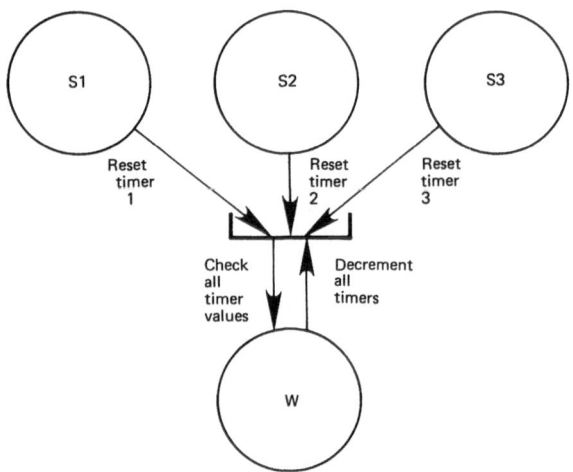

Figure 5.3 Watchdog timer

Redundant Information

Most systems will include deliberate, or implied, redundant information. Audit processes can make use of this redundancy. The system state implied by one pool can be checked against the system state implied by the information contained in another pool. An audit process will flag an error if it finds two versions of system state information to be inconsistent.

Hardware Status

A common source of error lies in the fact that the state of the controlled system is not accurately reflected by the data structures in the software. This is especially true in the case of electromechanical controlled systems. An auditing process can check the state of devices (relays, switches, connected remote terminals, etc.) in the controlled system and can compare it with the state indicated by the information held in the relevant system data pool.

Should a discrepancy occur, an error could be flagged or, more simply, the pool state information updated. These auditing processes are particularly useful in systems where breakdowns and repairs are likely to result in parts of the controlled system being taken out of, or put into, service. Auditing processes can keep system state information up to date.

Note that machine instruction, code module and process level checks detect errors at, or close to, the time they occur. Audit level checks detect errors by the side effects they cause in the system data structures. These checks are therefore slower detection mechanisms. None the less, there will usually be sufficient redundant information in the system data pools to justify the existence of low-priority audit processes that continually check the consistency of this data.

5.3.5 System Level

In order to implement fault detection at the highest level, it is necessary to observe the system from an external viewpoint. This perspective is provided either by additional system hardware, or by a completely independent real-time system. The idea is to provide an observer totally detached from the observed system. For example, most mechanical systems include safety or fail-safe devices like governors, relief valves, etc. Electrical systems include voltage regulators and fuses. The activation of these devices would indicate a fault in either the controlled system or the controlling software. In either case, they can be used to trigger an alarm to the fault recovery system.

Not only must the observer be totally independent of the system being observed, but also it must be possible to differentiate between a fault in the observed system and a fault in the observing system.

Unexpected inactivity of a real-time system is often a symptom of faulty behaviour. For example, a common method of detecting failure in a teleprocessing centre is to include hardware to observe electrical activity on outgoing lines. Should all lines simultaneously become inactive for a number of seconds, a fault in the controlling software will be suspected.

Not all real-time systems work in isolation. In fact an increasing number of systems are members of sets of systems distributed on a communications network. In these instances other systems in the network can provide an external monitor of a system's behaviour. Here a time-out mechanism is helpful. Each network member would be expected to communicate with its neighbours with a certain regularity. If a system does not respond to an

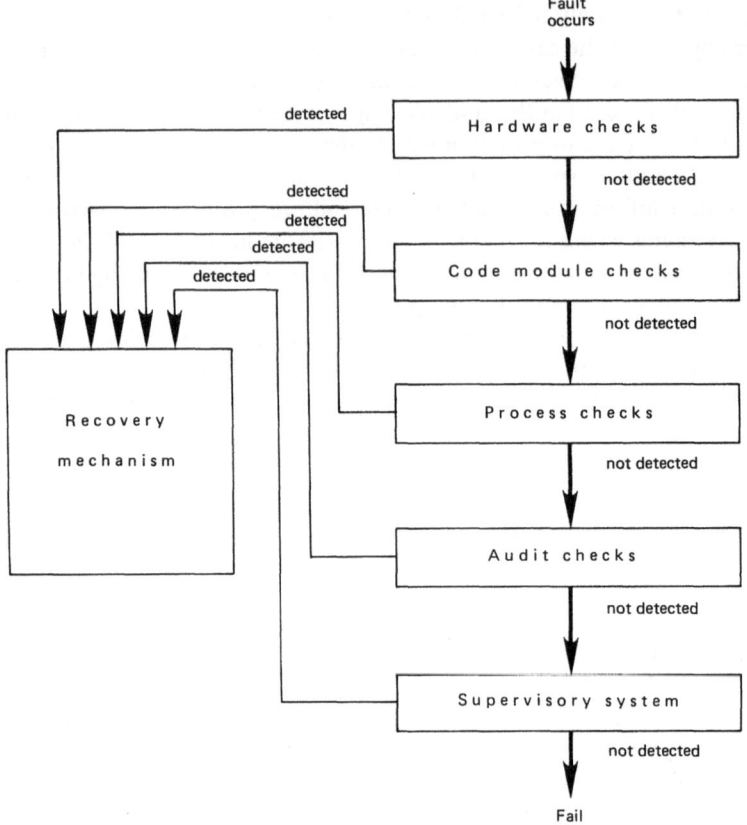

Figure 5.4 Fault detection

enquiry from a majority of its immediate neighbours within a pre-determined period of time, a malfunction within it or its neighbours can be assumed.

In summary then, we can envisage a hierarchy of fault detection mechanisms, all signalling the discovery of possible faults to a fault recovery mechanism. Figure 5.4 summarises the situation.

5.4   FAULT RECOVERY

Once the fault has been detected and signalled to the recovery monitor, it is up to that monitor to attempt to recover the system from the error. If correct operation cannot be continued, then the mechanism should, at the very least, ensure that the maximum error-diagnostic information is supplied to maintenance personnel before the system fails completely.

Initially we shall discuss a simple approach to system recovery, but we will also discuss some of the problems that this simple method tends to ignore.

5.4.1 Simple Approach

Early commercial data-processing systems often carried out lengthy calculations on hardware of questionable reliability. The following method was developed to avoid the necessity of repeating what could potentially run to hours of processing time.

Checkpoints

The programs were organised to create a series of checkpoints or footprints. These checkpoints were summaries of the current state of processing and were regularly placed on backing store. Whenever a fault was detected, the program needed only to be 'rolled back' to the last checkpoint before restarting. The checkpoints acted as a series of milestones. When each milestone was passed, the program was known to be acting correctly. This strategy can be readily applied to the real-time environment.

Figure 5.5 represents the flow of control in a hypothetical process code element. Many processes exhibit a circular control path, as shown in the diagram. However, even if the process is initiated at point A and terminated at point D, the following discussion will still apply.

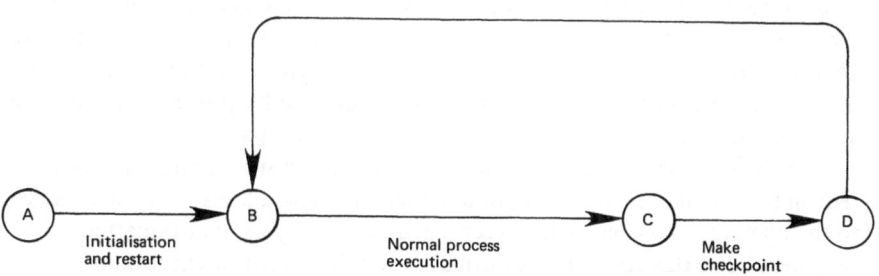

Figure 5.5 Process flow

When the process is first activated, it carries out initialisation activities. These may consist of checksum validation of correct loading of the code element, initialisation of variable values and, in the case of a process controlling a physical device, initialisation of the device (for example, positioning a disc arm). The data used to initialise variables, status words and device status information are not fixed, but read from a checkpoint data area. Ideally this data area is held in a highly protected area of memory or, better still, on backing store.

After the initialisation is completed, the process enters its main body of processing. On completion of one cycle of process execution, the current value of variables, status words, etc., are stored in the checkpoint data area. The process may then terminate or, more usually, return to point B for a second cycle.

Imagine, now, that an error has been discovered and the recovery monitor has been informed. The monitor will halt the process and cause it to be rolled back to its most recent checkpoint. To do this the monitor need simply restart the process at point A, having reloaded the code element of the errant process into main storage. The process will then continue from its checkpoint.

The faulty process does not, of course, exist in isolation. All processes associated with the faulty process will notice, either directly or via auditing mechanisms within the channel/pool monitors, that the process is acting irregularly. Signals will then be sent to the recovery monitor. The irregularities will initially be caused by the faulty behaviour of the process but, for a period of time after the process is rolled back, irregularities will still be detected. This is because the process, by being rolled back, has had its normal sequence of operation changed and is therefore not behaving as the neighbouring processes expect. They will still signal errors. To avoid this unstable situation the reliability monitor will be designed to ignore error signals stimulated by recently rolled-back processes until such time as the subsystem surrounding the process has had time to settle down.

If, after a pre-determined period of time, the process is still causing error signals, it can be assumed that the process producing signals is not the culprit. The problem will more likely lie in a nearby process. In this case, the whole neighbouring subsystem is rolled back. Again, the reliability monitor would ignore error signals from surrounding subsystems for a specified time period. If the error persists, then the whole system will be rolled back and restarted. Also, depending on the application area and on system performance requirements, it may be possible for the reliability monitor to abort faulty processes or subsystems and have the system continue operation at a reduced capability.

Should the error persist to the extent that the system could no longer remain operational, then alarms could be raised. These alarms could be messages to the operator's console, lights, sirens, bells, etc. Diagnostic information could be generated at this stage. This information would consist of execution summaries, snapshot dumps of parts of memory (see section 8.3.2.1), register contents and the status of hardware devices. The information would be dumped to backing store, high-speed hard-copy device or the operator's console.

This simplified approach to rollback makes a basic assumption. It implies that the faulty operation of the system was caused by a peculiar set of circumstances that will not readily recur once the system is rolled back. In many cases this is a valid assumption and, in the interests of keeping the system as simple as possible, it would be advisable to use this approach until it has been proven inadequate. We have, however, brushed over a number of significant problems. It is well that we consider them.

5.4.2 More Complex Recovery Methods

Redundant Modules

If the conditions that caused a piece of software to fail occur again, then naturally the software will continue to fail. The only way to attempt to cure the fault is to alter the software. As we mentioned before, it is usual for hardware reliability systems to include redundant modules. This technique can be used in software. Rather than roll back the current code element, a different code element is used. The replacement module will, of course, be designed to do the same job as the original module.

Obviously, the redundant code module will not be exactly the same as the currently running module. In the simplest case, the redundant code element could be an earlier version of the current module. Often, the correction of errors inadvertently introduces new errors and the use of a previous version of the software may clear the fault. A more satisfactory alternative would be to use a completely independent module. This module would have been produced to exactly the same design specification, but probably by a different programmer or team of programmers. As soon as the original code element has been corrected it is re-introduced into the system, replacing the backup module. The rationale behind this strategy is that the original module has been in service for a longer period and therefore undergone more 'in-service testing'. In this way the original module becomes more and more reliable as time goes by and the errors are corrected. It must be stressed at this stage that this, like any other technique that implies the production of redundant elements, is expensive.

Recovery Blocks

In our simple system a process has only one checkpoint. There is, of course no reason why it could not be broken into a number of code elements, each with its own checkpoint (and redundant code element for that matter). This situation is shown in figure 5.6. Clearly the major drawback of this approach is the overhead of storing checkpoint information. Randell (1975) has suggested a formal solution to this problem. He uses a type of assertion mechanism in

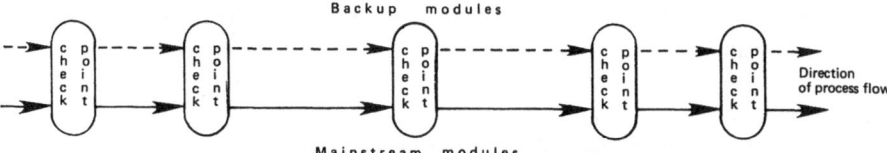

Figure 5.6 Multiple checkpoints

conjunction with a mechanism for storing checkpoint information. These mechanisms are invisible to the programmer.

A program is divided into *recovery blocks* headed by acceptance tests. The recovery blocks consist of a number of alternative code blocks, headed by a primary 'alternative'. Checkpoint is stored prior to entering a recovery block information. The primary 'alternative' is then entered and executed. Before the block is exited, the acceptance test (a boolean expression) is evaluated. If the test succeeds, the block is exited. If not, the situation is reset to the point where the block was entered and the second 'alternative' will be executed. Successive 'alternatives' are tried until the acceptance test is passed, or no further 'alternatives' are available, in which case default error code is executed.

The recovery block concept provides a convenient model for use in the design of the recovery structure of individual processes; however, real-time constraints may arbitrate against employing too complex a recovery structure. Storage of checkpoint information at the entrance to each block may impose too heavy an overhead. If this technique is to be used, it may be necessary to restrict the depth of recovery block nesting.

Conversations

In both the simple approach and the recovery block approach, we return to a checkpoint by resetting the system to the state prevailing at the time the checkpoint was passed. This action is facilitated by a simple assignment of prior values to data variables.

We have ignored the problem of irreversible processes. Consider a process that causes the reading of a card in a card reader. In order to roll back this process it is necessary to 'unread' a card. This is patently impossible. We have also ignored the problem of process interaction. What should be done if a process fails after receiving and destroying information from one process, and sending incorrect information to a third process? The failure and rollback of the central process implies the need for the neighbouring process also to be rolled back. Randall has suggested a design tool to be used in minimising these problems. He introduces a structure called a *conversation*, which provides a recovery structure common to a set of interacting processes.

Figure 5.7 represents a recovery block where the downward-pointing arrow indicates the over-all progress of the process. The top edge of the square corresponds to the environment of the process on entry — the checkpoint information. The bottom edge represents the acceptable state of the process, as checked by an acceptance test, when it exits from the recovery block. The sides show that the recovery block is independent, from a recovery viewpoint, of any other activity operating in the system.

Now if we include part of the progress of another process in the same recovery block we have what is termed a *conversation*; see figure 5.8. We specify that all the processes must satisfy their respective acceptance tests before any

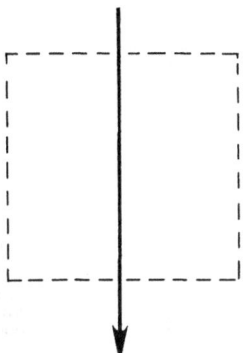

Figure 5.7 Recovery block

may proceed beyond their test point. If any of the processes fail their test, all the processes must be rolled back to their individual checkpoints, where they entered the conversation.

The term 'conversation' is apt for this structure since, while in the conversation recovery block, member processes may not communicate or interact with processes outside the conversation. Conversations may be nested, but may not intersect.

Figures 5.9 and 5.10 show conversations for the two examples of irreversible processes described above. In order to implement the conversation facility, it would be necessary to include calls to the system's interprocess synchronisation mechanisms (WAIT and SIGNAL).

Recovery blocks and conversations are valuable design aids. An ideal situation would be for the checkpoint creation and recovery mechanism to be transparent to the designer and implemented as part of the language compiler. However, even if these mechanisms are not available, the structure they recommend is in itself a useful tool for the designer when he is considering a recovery strategy for his system.

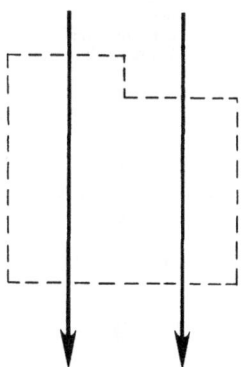

Figure 5.8 Conversation

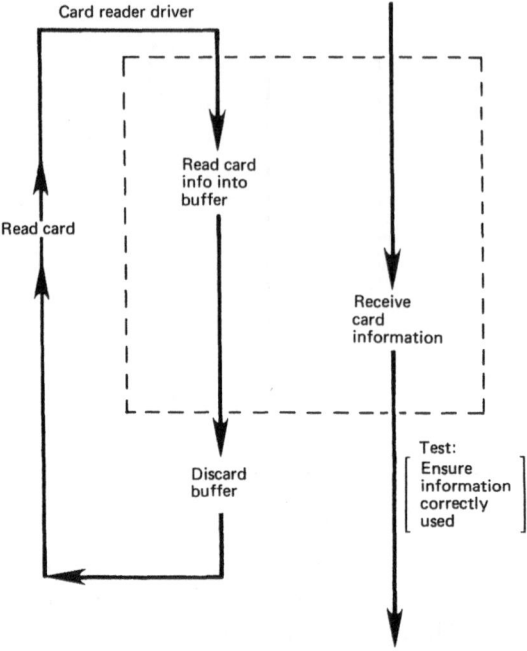

Figure 5.9　Card reader process and consumer process

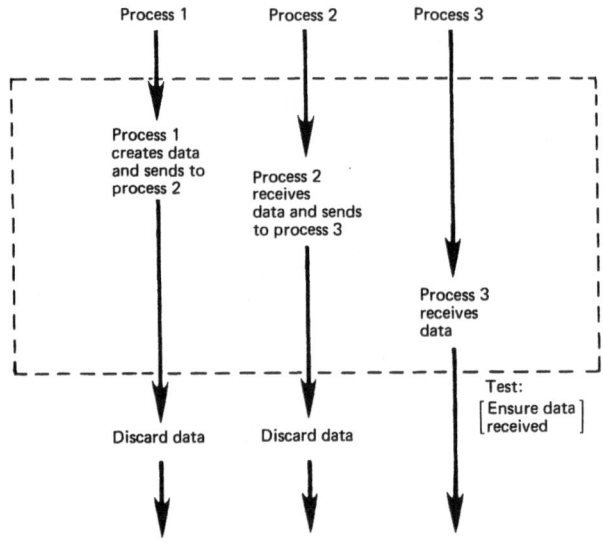

Figure 5.10　Three processes communicating a piece of data

5.5 RECOVERY LEVELS

So far we have discussed a number of error-detection and recovery mechanisms which would be valuable should one of the system processes malfunction. For the recovery system to be complete, however, it must be able to recover from faults occurring within the recovery system itself. After all, there is no special reason why the recovery monitor, for example, should be exempt from failure. To overcome this problem, the virtual machine concept proves effective once again. We shall structure the recovery system in such a way that it provides successive layers of increasingly reliable environments. Each level will monitor the operation of the succeeding layer by means of a watchdog timer.

5.5.1 The Hardware Level

We have already assumed that the hardware design includes error-detection and correction facilities. In order to highlight any faults in the hardware, we introduce a process that does nothing but exercise the hardware. It is used to execute the repertoire of CPU instructions, write bit patterns to memory, etc. If well designed, the process should be short and exercise the hardware thoroughly This process has as its watchdog the real-time clock interrupt. Should the process not reset its timer, the hardware bootstrap program will re-initialise the process. To allow for the possibility of a failure in the real-time clock, the independent system level watchdog can be used as a backup stimulus to the exerciser.

The hardware exerciser provides a reliable environment where correct operation of the hardware can be assumed. The process acts as a watchdog to the code tester process.

5.5.2 The Instruction Code Level

The code tester performs a dual function. By reading a process's code into its allocated space in memory it acts as a conventional process code loader. It also performs correctness tests on the code once it is loaded, such as checksum tests. This reliability level ensures that process code has been correctly loaded. The code tester process acts as a watchdog to the recovery monitor and the wait/signal process.

5.5.3 The Code Module Level

The recovery monitor lies at the focus of the reliability system and receives indications of malfunctions from both higher and lower reliability levels. It is the recovery monitor that implements process checkpointing and recovery block activities. By including the recovery monitor we ensure an orderly recovery from errors in code modules and thus assure a reliable environment at this level.

In order that code sharing and recovery block conversations can be carried out, it is also necessary to guarantee a correctly operating wait/signal operation at this level. The wait/signal processes act as watchdog to the channel/pool monitors.

5.5.4 The Process Level

The channel and pool monitors attempt to ensure correct operation of system processes by monitoring their external behaviour. If necessary, the monitors can be designed to include a watchdog timer facility, or special watchdog processes can be set up for the purpose. At this level we provide an environment where the reliability of processes can be assured as far as is possible. Auditing processes can then be introduced to check the consistency and correctness of sets of processes within the system.

For a successful, functioning example of this form of reliability hierarchy the reader is referred to the ARPANET Pluribus Imp System, detailed in chapter 6.

5.6 RECOVERY PRIORITY

5.6.1 Fixed Priority

The previous discussion has made the tacit assumption that the recovery monitor will instigate recovery action the moment a fault is discovered. This implies that the monitor will be the highest-priority process in the system. It is vital the fault be prevented from propagating further and affecting other parts of the system. Faults have a habit of spreading very rapidly and it is very dangerous to ignore them. Giving the recovery monitor the highest priority is a sound practice.

5.6.2 Variable Priority

While bearing in mind the points made in the previous paragraph, the tactic of having a recovery monitor of very high priority is not necessarily ideal in all cases. While the CPU is engaged in executing recovery proceedings, it is unavailable for use in advancing normal system operation. When the system is in a time-critical situation it may well be better for a minor fault to go temporarily unheeded, and recovery postponed, while important processing is performed. Once the system workload slackens, recovery can be instigated.

Faults will normally be signalled to the recovery system via a software trap. The trap-handling process can be designed to note the fault, disable the offending process, update any relevant system status pools and perform a brief analysis as to the seriousness of the fault. At this point, this process could adjust the priority of the recovery monitor before exiting to the dispatcher. Recovery action would then take place at a time related to its importance.

A better and more consistent approach is to centre the allocation of priority with the high-level scheduler. Recall from chapter 4 that part of the duties of the high-level scheduler is to dynamically adjust process priority so that the system may react correctly to an overload situation. Very often, the occurrence of a fault will result in system overload. A fault will reduce the system's performance capability while it is present, and increase the load by the necessary recovery activities. So, even if the system workload remains static during the fault, an overload may occur. Moreover, it is often the case that the system workload rises after a fault because of the buildup of a backlog of work to be done. This condition is particularly acute in systems which co-operate with others.

The problems of allocating process priority during recovery and during overload situations are intertwined. It is sensible, then, to combine the operations in a high-level scheduler. If we do this, the software trap handler that handles fault traps would not alter the recovery monitor's priority, but rather transfer indication of the seriousness of the fault to the high-level scheduler.

5.7 EXAMPLE

For our example, we will use a very simple recovery scheme. Each process is assumed to use one checkpoint, in the manner described in section 5.4.1 and to have a control path as shown in figure 5.5. To instigate recovery it is necessary to restart the process at point A; see figure 5.5. To be able to do this we must have saved the volatile environment as it stands when the process is at point A. The logical place to store this information is in the process descriptor. So, yet again we extend the process descriptor to include the volatile environment of the process at its starting point. Another kernel queue will be necessary, the FAULTY queue.

Should a fault be detected, it will be indicated to the kernel via a trap. The trap handling process acts as follows

Fault Trap
(1) Lock out interrupts
(2) Insert RUNNING into FAULTY
(3) Unlock interrupts
(4) SIGNAL fault
(5) Exit to dispatcher.

The recovery monitor will WAIT on a semaphore *fault*. The recovery monitor acts as follows

> *Recovery Monitor*
> (1) WAIT on fault
> (2) Transfer initial status to volatile environment in the process descriptor at the HEAD of the FAULTY queue
> (3) Remove ELEMENT from FAULTY then insert ELEMENT into RUNNABLE
> (4) Go back to (1).

5.8 SUMMARY

At this stage we should be in a position to create a system that is as correct and as reliable as possible. No complex system can be totally reliable. This is especially true of real-time software systems where, in the next minute, hour or month of operation, an untested or unexpected circumstance will occur, causing the system to fail. There are two main approaches to maximising system reliability: first, by using highly structured software and a thorough testing scheme, to minimise the residual errors in the software; second, to create fault-tolerant systems that can continue operation in the presence of errors. The first approach should be used in *every* system. The second is expensive, but it should be used as well whenever economically feasible.

To summarise our discussion to date, it may be convenient to think of the processes in a real-time system as having positions in a hypothetical three-dimensional space. In one dimension we have the level of the process in the real-time virtual machine hierarchy, in another the process's priority and in the third the process's level in the reliability hierarchy.

Concepts

System availability; mean time between failure; mean time to repair; fault tolerance; protective redundancy; audit processes; watchdog timers; rollback; checkpoints; recovery blocks; conversations

6 Design Methodology

In chapters 2 to 5 we introduced and discussed the form and construction of a real-time virtual machine. Although we have provided the designer with a useful tool, we have not provided him with a finished design. In his role as designer, he must still define the layout of processes, channels and pools, and specify the internal structure of the processes concerned. In this chapter we shall take an abstract look at the entire design process, in an attempt to discover some useful design techniques. Later, in chapter 7, we shall investigate techniques utilised in the creation of the internal structure of the real-time processes.

Design

The fundamental aim of all designers is to produce a 'good' design. A good design in a software environment will result in a product which does the job — one that satisfies the requirement and performance specifications and is as reliable and as easy to maintain as possible. The basis of good software design can be summarised in two basic concepts — correspondence and simplicity. Correspondence guarantees correctness and simplicity ensures reliability and maintainability.

6.1 CORRESPONDENCE

The secret to the design of correct, maintainable software lies in the creation of a software structure which corresponds to the structure of the problem at hand.

If the data structures, and the instructions that act on them, describe a model whose form reflects that of the application, any changes in the behaviour of the application can be readily incorporated in the software. Unless the process/channel/pool layout accurately reflects the interaction of activities in the application, and the modular design of the processes themselves reflects the internal structure of the activities, an inelegant and inflexible design will result.

Often a great deal of analysis will be required to delineate the underlying structure of the application, and the true structure will not be the one evident on first inspection. Great care must be taken at this early stage, for an error at the system-design phase will nullify any advantages gained by using well-structured program code or local optimisations of execution speed.

To reiterate, software design involves specification of the data structures and the functions that act on them. Some design methods approach the problem from the direction of the functions, while others focus the design on the data structures. We will first discuss the functional approach.

6.1.1 Top-down Functional Design

The usual approach to most large engineering problems is to effect a top-down modular decomposition of the problem. Top-down design involves breaking a problem down into smaller and smaller parts (or modules) to a point where each individual part is comprehensible and can be implemented. It is basically the 'divide-and-conquer' technique used in most problem-solving activities. The virtual machine that we have designed facilitates this approach.

The first step in a top-down functional design for a real-time system is to divide the system into processes. For this to be done precisely, the interfaces between processes, and the function of each process, must be clearly defined. Then each process is itself broken down into subsections; the function of each subsection and the interfaces between them are again, closely defined. A successful top-down design will result in a hierarchy of closely defined modules, each module being small enough to be implemented as 20 to 60 lines of program code. This is the maximum size that a program can be before it starts to become incomprehensible.

Unfortunately, difficulties are often encountered, and the use of this technique does not automatically imply a clean design. These difficulties do not stem from the top-down technique itself, but from difficulties in correctly breaking the problem into modules. Successful functional design is best learnt by experience, but all the same a number of guidelines can prove helpful.

First, a top-down design must be iterative. The designer must be prepared, indeed willing, to retrace his steps up the design tree and redefine certain steps in the decomposition. He must do this if he finds that the structure of lower-level modules does not correspond to the structure of the function in the problem area.

Second, where practical, important design decisions should be put off as far down the design tree as possible. Obviously, by the time a large system has been completely broken down into implementable modules most, if not all, of the design decisions will have been made. However, the earlier in the design a particular decision is made, the greater will be the influence of that decision on the final design. For instance, by using our real-time virtual machine, it is possible to work a long way down the design path of each process before having to make any decisions as to the processor/memory configuration. If modules that require specific hardware characteristics are relegated to the lowest level of the design tree, the final design could be implemented on a variety of hardware configurations If, on the other hand, a decision made at an early stage in the design compromised this versatility, a much less flexible product would result.

It is often not at all clear which modular breakdown best corresponds to the structure of the problem. Different designers may well produce different breakdown schemes for the same problem. Constantine (1974) has suggested that the relative quality of different breakdown schemes for one particular problem can be based on considerations of module *cohesion* and *coupling*. While these concepts do not provide explicit guidelines for successful modularisation, they are valuable for purposes of comparison of different designs.

6.1.1.1 Cohesion

Cohesion describes how well or naturally the module holds together — its internal strength. Proceeding from a low level of cohesion, which implies poor internal structure, to a high level of cohesion, we have

(1) coincidental cohesion, where the components are in the module purely by coincidence;
(2) logical cohesion, where the module performs a set of independent but logically similar functions, for example, a set of different print routines;
(3) temporal cohesion, where the module performs a set of functions that are related in time, for example, system start-up routines;
(4) procedural cohesion, where the functions in the module correspond to the sequence of functions appearing in a section of program;
(5) communicational cohesion, where functions operating on common data are grouped together;
(6) sequential cohesion, where the functions in the module co-operate to modify a piece of data; typically, such a module would accept data from one module, modify it and pass it on to another module;
(7) functional cohesion, where every function in the module contributes the performance of a single task.

Functional, sequential and communicational cohesion are most desirable, whereas temporal, logical and coincidental cohesion are much less desirable. Note that our design of the real-time virtual machine encourages the design of processes with high functional, sequential and communicational cohesion.

6.1.1.2 Coupling

Coupling is a relative measure of the strength and complexity of module interconnection. Ideally there should be a minimum amount of coupling between modules. It should be possible to remove a module from the system and replace it with a new modified module without affecting the over-all system in any way. If this is so, then the ideal of easy maintenance is furthered. By reducing intermodule connections and defining modules that are, as far as possible, free standing, the designer stands a better chance of being able to replace modules with minimum disruption at a later date.

Whereas processes communicate via channels and pools, modules internal to processes interface with the rest of the module by control mechanisms and via data-transfer mechanisms. Take, as an example, module B in figure 6.1 Module B's control interfaces are: called by A, calls C and D. Its data interfaces are: parameters passed while being called by A, parameters passed when calling C and D, and process-wide data areas to which B has access. Ideally we should be able to remove B from the system and replace it with a modified version or, expressed another way, we should be able to change A or C or D, or the form of the global data, without affecting B. Hide from B any information that it does not have to know and we reduce B's coupling to the rest of the system.

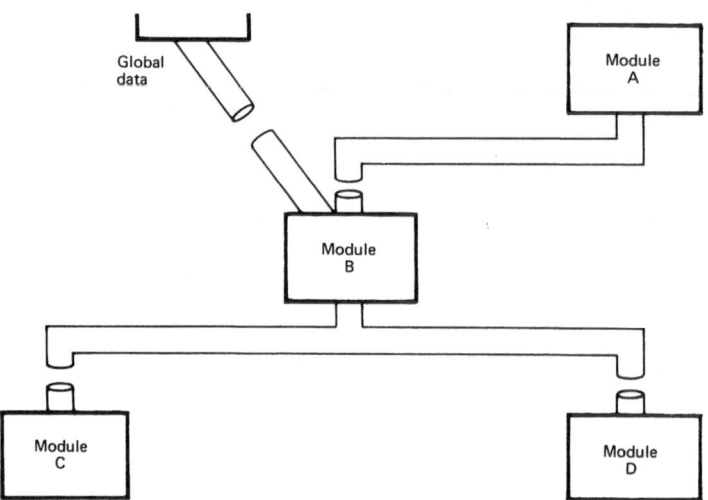

Figure 6.1 Module coupling

Consider B's data interface. Module B will need to read from or write to global data areas. Presumably it uses the information to modify its actions or those of the process. Normally it will require only the value of the information and will be unconcerned as to how it is stored. Provided these values can be written or read, B will perform correctly. If B uses standard routines to read and write the information, it need have no knowledge of the layout of the global area. This means that the layout of the global data can be changed without affecting the action of B at all. If, however, B was aware of the global data layout, and used this knowledge, any change in the layout would imply the need for a change in B.

Let us now consider the data interface with the other modules. If the total interaction between B and A, C, D operates by means of parameters passed during subroutine calls, B, A, C and D may be altered in any way, provided they still transfer the expected parameter values to the other modules. Consider an example. Module A passes module B an array of integers for sorting. This is all module A need know about the workings of module B. As a result of B's action, module A does not expect other effects to manifest themselves in the transferred data. If the designer of A expects side effects to occur, because of his knowledge of module B's design, an informal, undocumented connection is created between the modules. At a later date, B may be re-designed and no longer cause the side effects that A expects. The result — unreliable software.

When discussing the harmful effects of high coupling, Bergland (1978) quotes a telling analogy attributable to Alexander. He considers a system of 100 light bulbs, each of which can be either on or off. The bulbs are connected such that, if a light is on, it has a 50 per cent chance of going off in the next second. If it is off, but connected to other bulbs, it has a 50 per cent chance of going on in the next second, provided that one of the lights to which it is connected is on. If none of the lights connected to it is on, the bulb remains off. Eventually, the system will reach a state of equilibrium where all lights are off.

Now, if the lights are totally unconnected, the equilibrium state will on average be reached in the time it takes one light to go off. This is approximately two seconds. If we take the case where every bulb is connected to every other bulb, equilibrium would be reached in 10^{22} years! If, however, the lights were fully interconnected within independent sets of 10 bulbs, equilbrium would be reached in approximately 17 minutes. In software terms the last example would be equivalent to a set of highly cohesive modules with low intermodule coupling.

6.1.2 Information Hiding and Data Abstraction

A common mechanism in military information systems is the 'need-to-know' principle. Each person is given only as much information as he needs to know in order to carry out his function correctly. This policy is an ideal one to follow when designing a module: hide as much information as possible away from the module. In this way the coupling between modules, and therefore the complexity of the system, can be reduced.

Information hiding at the process level is aided and abetted by the use of channel and pool monitors. A process does not 'see' the data structure in a channel or pool directly; it only sees an abstract model of the structure, as provided by the monitor's access routines. This principle of data abstraction is fundamental to most modern design methodologies.

6.1.3 Data Structure Design Method

Top-down functional decomposition does not automatically result in program structure that exhibits close correspondence to the problem at hand. This is because it is often difficult to create a model of the problem by initially defining the activities to be performed. However, if we first model the system *items* as data structures it becomes a more straightforward task. The items in the system are easy to identify, and the best way of modelling them is usually apparent. It is for this reason that the data structure design method begins by defining the data structures (Jackson, 1975).

The crux of the method is to make the structure of the environment dictate the structure of the data structures and, in turn, to make the structure of the data dictate the structure of the functions and the processes in the system. In this way, the functions will exhibit close correspondence to the problem environment. The correspondence between data structure and program structure can readily be seen at the program-code level. The basic program structuring components are the sequence, iteration (loop) and selection (decision); see figure 6.2. These structures have direct counterparts in basic data structures.

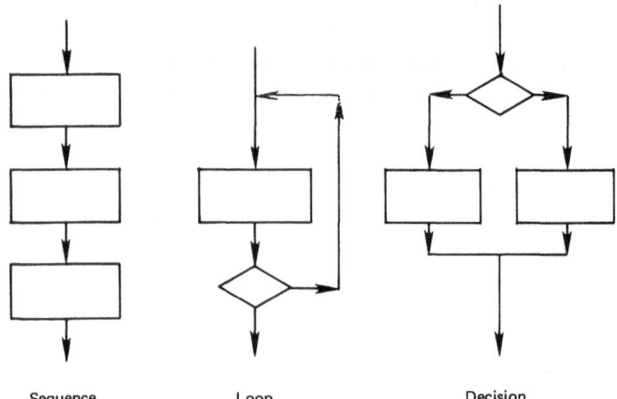

Sequence   Loop   Decision

Figure 6.2 Code structuring elements

The sequence

Data structure A consists of: Item B;
                                   Item C;
                                   Item D.

The iteration

Data structure A consists of: array(1 to index) of Item B.

The selection

Data structure A consists of: depending on selector
$$\text{if selector} = \text{first then Item B;}$$
$$\text{if selector} = \text{second then Item C;}$$
$$\text{if selector} = \text{third then Item D.}$$

Just as the action constructs can be nested, so the data structure constructs can be nested. Item B for instance, may be a sequence, iteration or selection. This correspondence between data structures and action structure is the key concept in the data structure design method.

To design the functional structure of a process, the designer proceeds as follows. First, he models the input and output data using the basic structures mentioned above. The designer should then be able to see elements in the output data structure that correspond to transformed elements in the input data structure. The purpose of the process is to effect these transformations. The program structure is a direct parallel of the structure of the data being manipulated. The designer does not need to invent the functional structure of the process; it is provided for him by the structure of the data. Sometimes, the input and output data structures are totally incompatible. It will then be necessary to introduce intermediate data whose structure lies midway between that of the input and output structures. The process then performs two functions: it transforms the input data to the intermediate form, then transforms this data to the requisite output form.

6.1.4 Real-time Software Design

Top-down functional design and data structure design approach the design problem from different angles. Both result in the design of data structures and functions, but one may be more applicable than the other in a particular set of circumstances. The decision as to which method is used is up to the designer's discretion. To date no universal design methodology has been formulated for real-time systems. We can, however, postulate a viable plan of attack, as follows

(1) Design and build a virtual machine that will support asynchronous co-operating processes. Previous chapters have discussed this task in detail.
(2) Identify all the items in the system and express them as data structures.
(3) Collect the data structures into pools and thus specify the processes that act on these pools.
(4) Specify any prerequisite synchronisation or information channels necessary for the processes to interact correctly.
(5) Use a data structure design method to create the process's structure.
(6) Express the data structures and process functions as high-level language programs.

If one incorporates the above steps in a design framework and then applies the framework to the production of software, the resultant code should correspond closely to the system under control.

6.2 SIMPLICITY

The best panacea for complexity is simplicity. The simplest designs are usually the best designs. Too often, designers implement a complex and ornate design in the mistaken belief that the more intricate or 'clever' it is, the more successful it will be. One has only to look into the world of nature to see that the simpler designs are often the most successful.

We have used a number of techniques to ensure that the structure of a real-time system is as simple as possible. Separating the different system activities into discrete processes makes the over-all structure of the system easy to grasp. By using highly modular, well-structured code we create processes that are clear and easy to comprehend.

6.2.1 Simplifying Real-time Systems

Once the system is pressed into service, timing problems may cause major difficulties. Each process may perform perfectly correctly in isolation, but faults will occur when the system as a whole reacts incorrectly to sequences of events in its environment. The cause of these faults can nearly always be narrowed down to problems with process scheduling and synchronisation.

If each process has its own hardware, and/or the system runs without interrupts to force unexpected process swapping, the whole question of scheduling and synchronisation is greatly simplified. These conditions imply that processes run to completion. If this is the case, the problem of synchronisation simplifies to that of ensuring that processes are only activated under certain circumstances. Scheduling simplifies to the job of avoiding deadlock over any shared resources.

6.2.2 The Pluribus Imp

The Pluribus Imp, the multimicroprocessor system used by nodes in the ARPANET, uses the above form of simplification to great effect (Ornstein *et al.*, 1975). There are thirteen CPUs, but they are not dedicated to unique processes. Rather, each processor, when it finishes executing a process, repeatedly interrogates a central list for further work. This list is a priority-ordered queue of process descriptors requiring activation. A process descriptor consists of a number which identifies the process and it corresponds to the process's priority in the system. Because processors frequently access the queue it becomes the source of potential system bottleneck. Accordingly, the queue is implemented as special-purpose hardware. When a process requires activation, its number is placed in the queue, to be picked up by the first available processor when it reaches the top of the queue. A single instruction allows the highest-priority task to be fetched from the queue. Another instruction allows a new task to be placed at the correct location in the queue. The queue device acts as the scheduler and for this reason is called the 'pseudo interrupt device'.

The responsiveness of the system will be governed by the process execution times. If all CPUs have just begun to execute the longest process, the process length will restrict the speed with which a new high-priority process can gain a processor. The longest time that a high-priority process can be kept waiting is 400 ms. Accordingly, no process in the system can exceed this execution time. In order to prevent system deadlock, each resource is given a priority. No process may gain use of, and therefore lock out, a resource if it has already locked out another resource of equal or lower priority.

6.2.3 Keep it Simple

The Imp is an example of a system running under severe real-time constraints, yet it is simple in its design. As a general principle the designer should, at the outset, ask himself if it is really necessary to include the more complex aspects of real-time software in his system.

Much of the discussion of the previous chapters centred around attempts to reduce the complexity of the additional system software whose inclusion is made necessary by constraints of hardware cost. The availability of increasingly sophisticated hardware elements at continually decreasing cost means that the cost—benefit relationships within real-time systems are constantly changing. Is it really necessary to multiplex a single processor? Is it necessary to have interrupts other than the real-time clock? Is it necessary to have the real-time clock at all? The designer must address all these questions with an eye to simplicity.

6.3 SUMMARY

The purpose of all software design methodologies is to produce simple designs whose structure corresponds closely to that of the problem at hand. The various design methodologies approach this ideal from different directions. Both the top-down functional decomposition method and the data structure design method reach a solution to the problem posed, but by different paths. Where one method may be suitable the other may not, and vice versa. Formal design methodologies provide a constructive and efficient framework; they in themselves do not guarantee a totally satisfactory design. The designer must learn to use them with care, always keeping the concepts of correspondence and simplicity well in mind.

Concepts

Correspondence; simplicity; top-down functional design; cohesion; coupling; information hiding; data abstraction; data structure design technique

7 The Process Virtual Machine

In the previous section we developed a virtual machine with which it is possible to define a real-time system as a collection of co-operating processes. Assuming that a designer has progressed to the point where he has defined the function of and interfaces between the requisite processes, the next step is to design the internal structure of the processes themselves.

To design these processes it is necessary to specify the data structures and the machine instructions that make up their code element. Early in the history of computer applications it was found that the design of such programs, when they extend for more than one hundred or so instructions, becomes a difficult and error-prone task. This difficulty arises from the fact that machine instructions model the repertoire of actions and simple storage elements that are built into the design of the hardware. They do not reflect the actions and data structures that would naturally and clearly model a particular process activity.

The traditional solution to this problem has been to create a suitable virtual machine, by superimposing a language translator on to the hardware. The language is designed to model the problem area. Hence the existence of COBOL in the commercial field, FORTRAN in the scientific field and PASCAL (Wilson and Addyman, 1978) and others in the real-time systems programming area. These languages attempt to provide virtual machines suited to particular application areas. There is no reason why other virtual machines, more closely tailored to a particular project, cannot be built if the necessary support software is provided. This chapter will briefly describe the process level virtual machine provided by a high-level language and then will discuss two types of special-purpose virtual machines.

7.1 THE HIGH-LEVEL LANGUAGE MACHINE

As with the real-time virtual machine, the process virtual machine must reflect the underlying structure of the application. The software component of any application consists of a model comprising data structures and the action procedures that manipulate them. A useful virtual machine must therefore facilitate the definition and creation of data structures as well as allowing a highly structured representation of action algorithms. Most modern high-level languages incorporate these facilities.

The various high-level languages designed for real-time application share similar structure. They allow the designer to

(1) define data structures, both in terms of the primitive data storage elements (bits, bytes and words), and in terms of more complex data structures defined previously in the program;
(2) declare that instances of predefined data structures exist and that access to and knowledge of these data structures is restricted to different parts of the program;
(3) define a hierarchy of modules, consisting of data and action sequences, that form a logical whole;
(4) describe the action sequences within modules in terms of structured loop, conditional and sequential blocks.

Currently there exist a great number of real-time high-level languages; however, attempts are being made to encourage standardisation. The US Department of Defense is specifying its standard language, while international bodies such as the CCITT are attempting to introduce their own. Of the many languages now in use, PASCAL is fast becoming a *de facto* standard.

7.1.1 High-level Languages vs Assembler Languages

Real-time software systems have traditionally been written in assembler level program code. The main argument in favour of this approach has been the time-critical nature of most real-time applications. Programs written by experienced assembler programmers are generally more 'efficient' in speed and memory space requirements than those programs produced by compiler translation.

Efficiency

The criticism most often levelled against high-level languages is that the code produced by the compiler is relatively inefficient. When considering small amounts of program code (say 100 to 200 lines) this will usually be the case. A compiler cannot be as astute as a human programmer and often cannot find minor, local optimisations in particular programs. As the program increases in length, however, it becomes more and more difficult for the human programmer to maintain a grasp of the over-all structure of the program. As the program grows more complex, so the programmer's ability to optimise lessens. The compiler, on the other hand, is unconcerned with program length and its optimisation activities operate with equal efficiency no matter how long the program. For a certain length of program, a programmer may produce twice as efficient code as a compiler. Nevertheless, for programs of moderate length, a modern compiler cannot hope to produce code as efficient as that of a programmer writing in assembler code.

Life cycle Costs

When compared over the entire life cycle of the product, the high-level language has considerable advantages over assembler language implementation. Applications can be coded far more rapidly in a high-level language. The code produced is clearer to read and therefore better documented, and is easier to debug, maintain and extend. Further, by producing well-structured high-level language code, where important decision and control points are highlighted, it is possible to implement a reasonably thorough testing scheme. The high-level language compiler and run-time system is able to do sufficient checking to avoid many of the pitfalls of assembler level programming. For example, it is not possible to inadvertantly transfer control outside the bounds of a subprogram, something all too possible in assembler level programming. Moreover, automatic array bounds checking can be implemented and automatic variable-type checking conducted. The programmer is, in many ways, protected from himself.

During the software maintenance phase, a product coded in a high-level language is, without doubt, more economical than one coded in assembler code. The properties of good self-documentation, clear modularity and explicit structuring, inherent in a well-disciplined high-level language program, are vital to speedy and economical maintenance. Over all, these considerations have led designers in a strong swing toward the use of higher-level languages in real-time software.

7.2 THE INTERPRETING MACHINE

As useful as a general-purpose high-level language may be, it is possible to create virtual machines even more closely tailored to the problem at hand — and create them with relative ease. The first example we will discuss is the interpretive code machine.

7.2.1 Interpreters

A compiler translates the sequence of actions specified by a high-level-language program into an equivalent machine code program. When the program thus generated is run, the processing hardware reads an instruction, interprets the instruction to mean that it must carry out a certain action, then executes that action. A piece of *software* that acts in this way, reading, interpreting and executing a sequence of coded instructions, is called an interpreter.

A software designer may discover that the behaviour required of a particular part of the application at hand breaks down into a number of specific, small, closely defined actions, carried out in differently ordered sequences throughout the application. For example, in a certain industrial application, the activities 'move left', 'move right', 'move forward', 'move back', 'grasp' and 'release' may occur in differing order throughout the application. Now, if he were able to program a virtual machine that executed programs couched in terms of the above six instructions, then the designer's job would be greatly simplified.

It is unlikely, however, that there would be available a high-level language that included as part of its instruction repertoire the specific actions required by a particular application. It is also very unlikely that it would be economically viable to create a special-purpose compiler for only one application. It may, however, be possible to implement an interpreter.

7.2.2 Implementing an Interpreter

Let us assume that a particular application breaks down into a small set of actions, say *A*, *B* and *C*, repeated in different sequences throughout the application. In order to create a virtual machine which will execute a program of these actions, the designer proceeds as follows.

Each action in the set of actions will be given a unique instruction code. Also, each action will have associated with it a program, written in a suitable language, which carries out the functions necessary to implement the action. The interpreter is designed to read an instruction code, decide which program corresponds to that instruction code and, then transfer control of execution to the beginning of that program. Upon their completion, each of the action programs will transfer control back to the interpreter. The interpreter then reads the next instruction code in the program of instruction codes and the cycle is repeated.

Figure 7.1 shows the data structures that could be used by a simple interpreter. The code to be interpreted consists of a sequence of eight-bit storage elements. The left-hand four bits of each element will be interpreted as an action. The right-hand four bits will be interpreted as a parameter to be used when carrying out the action.

Both sets of bits are interpreted as numbers and used as indexes for data tables. The *action code address table* contains the value of the start location of the program code that implements each possible action. In this case there are sixteen possible actions. The *actual parameter table* contains a set of parameters. Each action is given an instruction code which corresponds to its location in the action code address table. When each action is executed, the interpreter makes the parameter indicated by the right-hand four bits of the code available to the action program. The instruction pointer indicates which code is to be interpreted next. On each cycle of the interpreter it is incremented to point to the next code in sequence. Non-sequential jumps within the interpreted code can be implemented by allowing action programs to manipulate the instruction pointer.

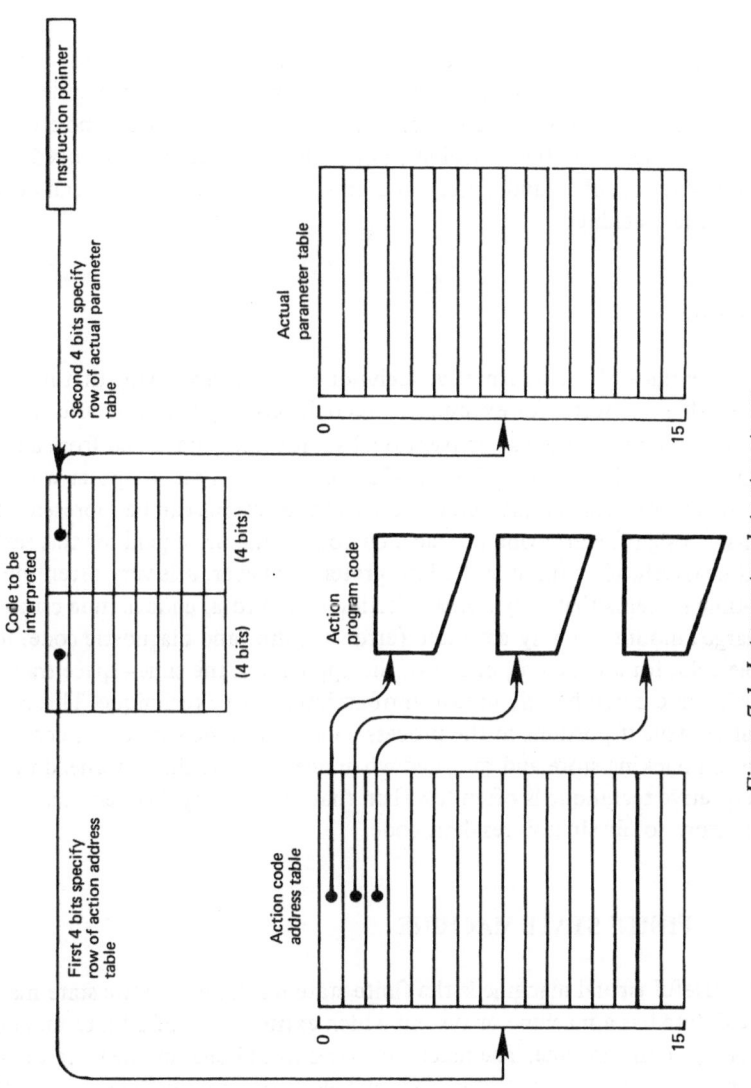

Figure 7.1 Interpreter data structures

7.2.3 Advantages of Interpreters

Flexibility

Once a designer builds the software necessary to create the data tables, and builds the interpreter itself, he is in a position to create a virtual machine tailored to part of the system he is designing. In fact, he is now in a position to create many different virtual machines. For each new machine all he need do is create a new set of tables and action programs. The same interpreter can be used in each of the machines.

Space Saving

A great advantage of the interpretive technique is the space saving that it engenders. If there were, for example, sixteen different possible actions, then they could be implemented as conventional subroutines and called from a main program. This method implies the use of at least one or two computer words per call. However, by using an interpreter, each of the actions can be represented by four bits — a significant saving in space. Of course, the price paid for this saving is the time overhead in running the interpreter. However, it is very often the case in real-time systems that only a small portion of the total code is time critical, and a large amount is rarely activated (error-handling and diagnostic code, for example). So, for a large proportion of the application the time—space tradeoff may well come down heavily in favour of an interpretive technique. This is particularly true if portions of the process code have to be stored, for economic reasons, on backing store and returned when needed. The time overhead in using an interpretive technique is often less than that imposed by frequent accesses to backing store to obtain non-resident code.

7.3   THE FINITE STATE MACHINE

Another useful virtual machine is the finite state machine. A finite state machine may be defined as a machine or system which exists in one of a finite number of states at any point in time. The machine moves from being in one state to being in another state as a result of some external event or stimulus. The state of the machine at any one particular time is a function of the previous history of the machine, together with the current stimulus. While the machine is moving from being in one state to another, it may carry out a sequence of actions.

Consider a very simple example. An electric motor has two control buttons marked 'start' and 'stop'. The motor can be in one of two states — on or off. Now, when the motor is off, two events can occur. The start button is pressed, or the stop button is pressed. If the stop button is pressed, the state of the motor remains the same — off. If the start button is pressed, the motor changes its state to on. If the current state of the motor is on, then pressing the stop button will result in a change of state to off; pressing the start button will not cause a change of state. Note that the future state of the motor is a function of its current state, together with any events that occur.

The 'state' nature of a machine is often represented graphically within a *state transition diagram*; see figure 7.2. In this diagram the states of the machine are represented as boxes with curved sides. For the machine to move from being in one state to being in another, some event must occur, signified here by a flag symbol. When passing from one state to another any actions carried out are represented by rectangular boxes; these will appear in later diagrams. This form of representation of a finite state machine is that recommended by the CCITT (1977), an international standards organisation, in their Specification and Design Language.

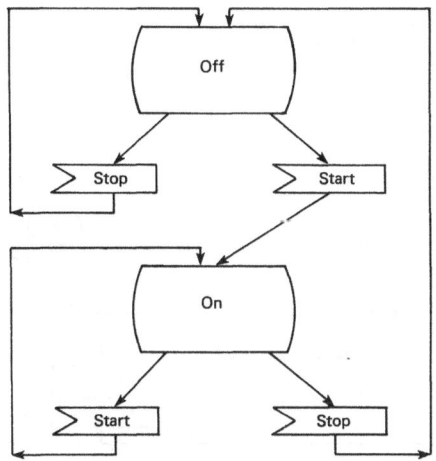

Figure 7.2 Simple state transition diagram

The electric motor is, of course, an extremely simple example. It is, however, possible to model many complex real-time applications as finite state machines. Consider the states of an individual call in a computer-controlled telephone exchange. The call passes from being in an idle state to awaiting dialled digits, ringing, talking, then terminating the call. A process that is sampling an input stream of characters and looking for certain patterns of data is another example. Such a process may be, for example, a syntax analyser for a compiler or text-translating process, or it may be the input process in a message switching or TELEX centre.

Consider the TELEX example. Let us assume that an input process is reading in messages. These messages consist of a string of characters. In actual systems the message would begin with the pattern ZCZC and end with the pattern NNNN. We could model the action of the input process as a finite state machine. An event in this case is the receipt of a character. This is shown in figure 7.3. Here we have made the simplifying assumption that the message starts with ZC and ends with NN.

The process remains in the idle state until such time as a Z character is received. Once Z is received the state changes to that of waiting for a C. Should any character other than a C be received, the state returns to idle — remember that ZC is the start of message sequence. Should, however, a C be received at this point, the state of the machine becomes that of receiving and storing a message.

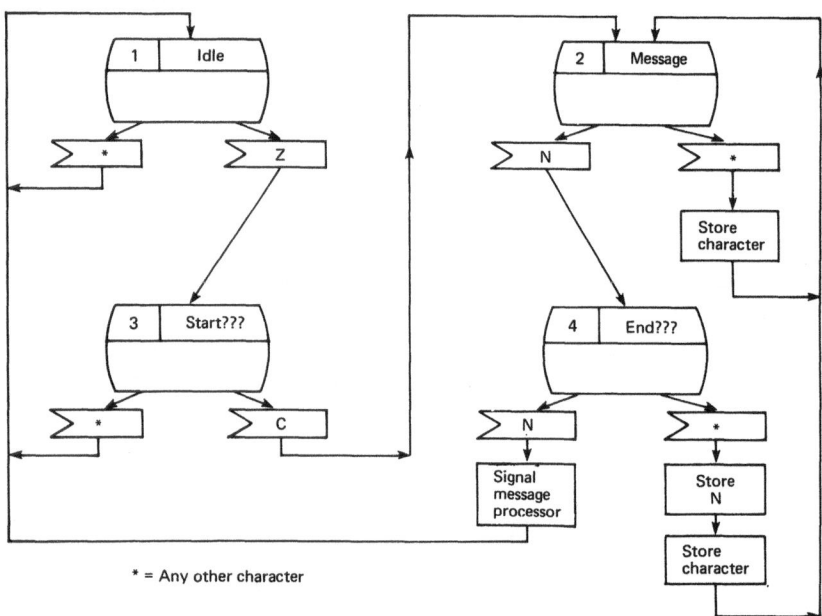

Figure 7.3 State transition diagram for message analyser

Should the process receive an N while in this state, then it may mean that the N is the first of the pair of Ns that signify the end message. Accordingly, the process changes state to that of awaiting the end of message. Should the next character again be an N, then the process designed to handle complete messages will be signalled, and the input process will return to a wait state. Should any other character be received, then it implies that the first N was simply part of the message text, so it is stored together with the current character and the process state becomes that of receiving a message.

7.3.1 Implementing a State Machine

If we assume that a finite state virtual machine would prove helpful, how can we create it in software? We shall investigate the implementation of a finite state machine in some detail in order to highlight the ease with which a powerful virtual machine can be created.

7.3.1.1 A Simple Approach

A first attempt would be to set up the data structures shown in Figure 7.4. The data structure is a simple mapping in tabular form of the information implicit in the state transition diagram. The *state table* has a row for each state in the machine. The row holds the number of the state, together with two integers which correspond to row numbers in the *action table.* These row numbers point to beginning and end rows of a section of the action table. Each section of the action table contains information about a particular state. Each row in the action table corresponds to an event which can occur; the action to be taken as a result of that event; and the state that the machine would enter on completion of the action. Figure 7.4 contains values corresponding to the state transition diagram in figure 7.3. The arrows in figure 7.4 show the situation if the machine were in state 1. The *current state* indexes the state table. The *begin* and *end* fields of row 1 of the state table indicate the section of the action table that represents state 1.

Once these tables are created the next step must be to construct a program which simulates the action of a state machine by acting on the information in the data structures shown in figure 7.4. The algorithm is quite straightforward

(1) *Get next event*
(2) Search down that part of the *action table* that corresponds to the current state, looking for the row corresponding to the event just received
(3) Carry out the action specified in the *action* column
(4) Set the current state register to the value in the *next state* column
(5) Go back to step 1.

The behaviour of the function *get next event* will depend on the system implementation. Its purpose is to provide the finite state machine with events in the order that they occur. If the finite state machine is implemented as a process in our real-time machine, then *get next event* will be a function which reads, from a channel, data representing events.

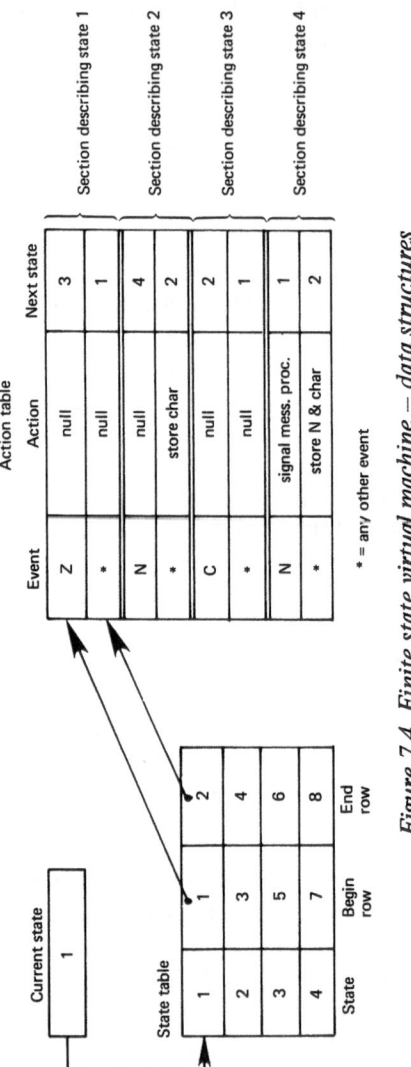

Figure 7.4 Finite state virtual machine — data structures

7.3.1.2 A More Useful Model

The above simple implementation implies that there is only one possible *next state* that can result from the occurrence of a particular event. This conforms to the formal mathematical definition of a finite state machine. However, when attempting to model real systems as state machines, it is frequently necessary to have more than one possible next state after the occurrence of an event. This is because the actions that result from the occurrence of an event may result in more than one outcome, which in turn may result in more than one set of actions and next states. Figure 7.5 shows an extremely simplified case of an on-line system that allocates a working buffer to each user. If, on the receipt of a 'log on' request. If it can allocate the buffer, then the user is logged on. Note that the outcome of the decision box is a function of the action 'allocate buffer'.

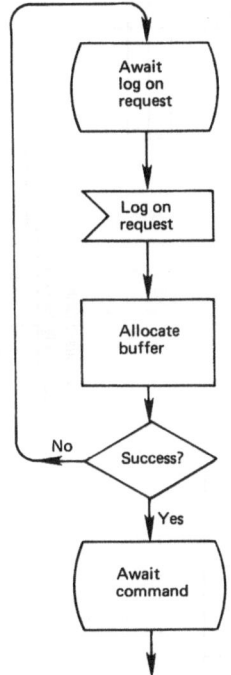

Figure 7.5 User log on scheme

To accomodate this situation we must refine the software model of a finite state machine. Because there is now possibly more than one next state for each current state—event combination, the state table must be extended to include an *auxiliary table*. The auxiliary table contains the additional action/next state information for those current state—event combinations which have more than one outcome. The state table must include a new column to store a flag which indicates whether the auxiliary table is to be used. In the following discussion, refer to figure 7.6. The auxiliary table would normally be an

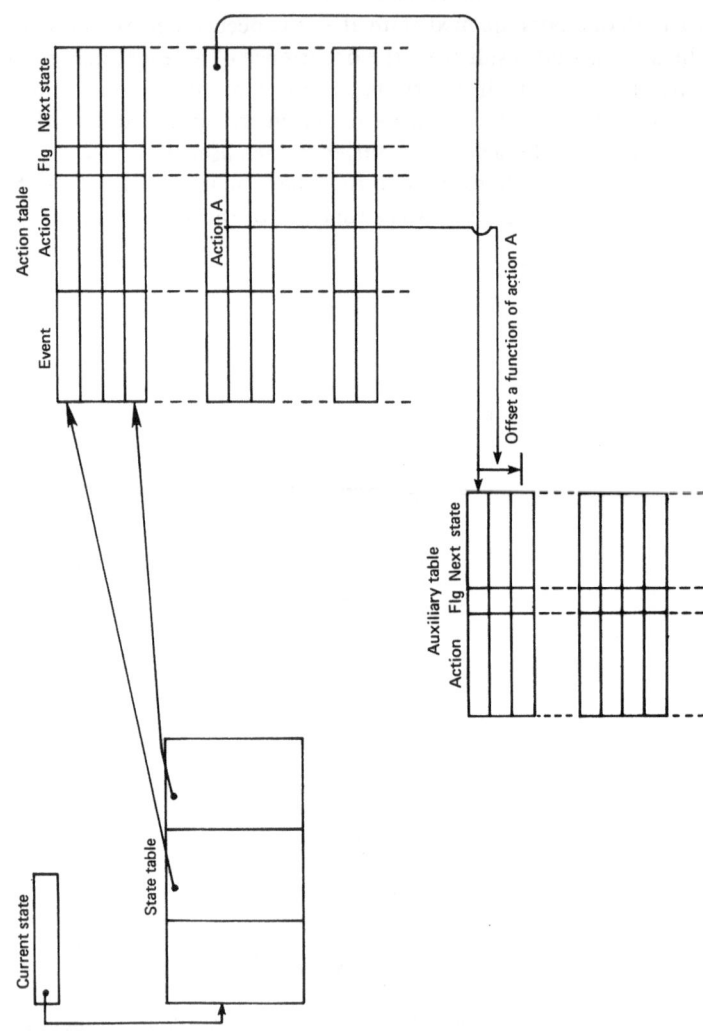

Figure 7.6 Finite state machine — extended data structures

extension of the state table; it is shown separately for clarity. Consider the following points.

(1) Every action procedure acts as a function, returning an integer value to the state machine's main procedure. This integer value corresponds to the outcome of the action and is a member of the contiguous set of positive integers, including zero. If an action has only one possible outcome, it will return to zero, if two outcomes zero or one; if three outcomes zero, one or two and so on.

(2) If the flag for a particular row is one, then the next-state field is interpreted as the next state. If the flag is zero, then the next state is interpreted as a pointer to the first row of a section of the auxiliary table.

(3) The auxiliary table is divided into sections consisting of a variable number of rows. Each row corresponds to the set of possible actions and next states that could eventuate when a particular action is carried out while the machine is in a particular state.

(4) The rows in the auxiliary table also include a flag bit, implying that actions in the auxiliary table could also lead to further actions and different next states.

The algorithm for the state machine program is now

(1) *Get next event*

(2) Search down that part of the action table which corresponds to the current state, looking for the event corresponding to the one just received

(3) Carry out the action specified in the action column of the current row

(4) If the flag bit *is* set, then set the current state register to the value in the next state column and go back to (1)

(5) Otherwise, add the value returned from this action function to the value in the next state field and use the result as an index to a row in the auxiliary table. Go back to (3), using this row index as the current row.

The event scanner   We have already mentioned that the *get next event* procedure will read events from an input channel. In the example shown in figure 7.4, an event is the receipt of a character, so the *get next event* procedure will read a stream of characters from the channel. But, of course, these characters or events must have been generated by some process at the other end of the channel. We shall call this process that generates events the *event scanner*.

Events are detected by scanning the system and comparing the present status with that found by the previous scan and reporting any differences as events. It is important that the events are passed to the finite state machine in the order in which they occur. Accordingly, careful event queueing will be necessary. Figure 7.7 shows a possible scenario. The event scanner reads the

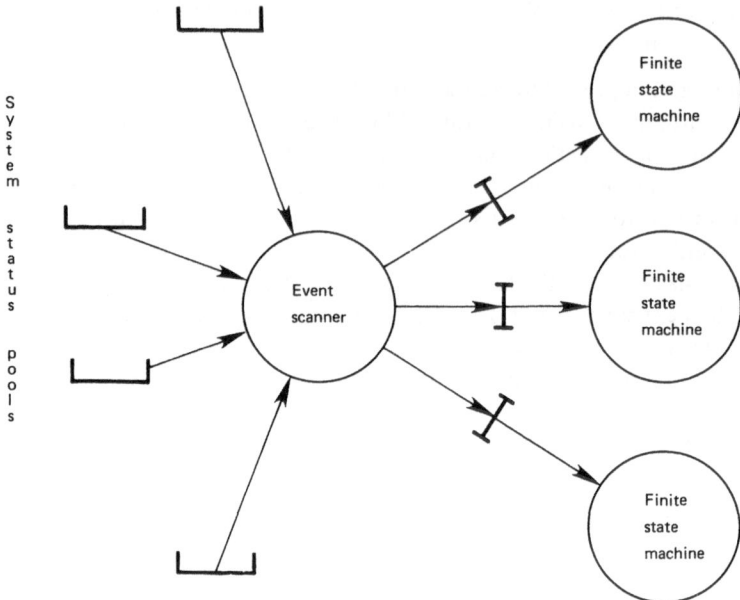

Figure 7.7 Event processor

status of the various system pools. If it detects any events, it channels them to the relevant finite state machine process. The channel would be implemented as a queue in this case, while the event could be an integer value passed down the channel.

Parallel machines in one process   Note in figure 7.7 that one event scanner is serving a number of finite state machine processes. It is possible to coalesce these state machine processes into one process which stimulates the action of a number of finite state machines running in parallel. To create such a process it is only necessary to extend the basic data structures and to provide action/ auxiliary tables for each of the machines in the process.

Rather than having a current state word, a *current state table* is provided. Each row in this table holds the current state of one of the machines in the process, together with a pointer to the machine's state table. The current state table is shown in figure 7.8. One extra integer is required to indicate which machine is in action at the current moment.

The message from the event scanner will also need extending to include an indication of the particular finite state machine to which the event refers. This could simply be an integer corresponding to the machine's row number in the current state table.

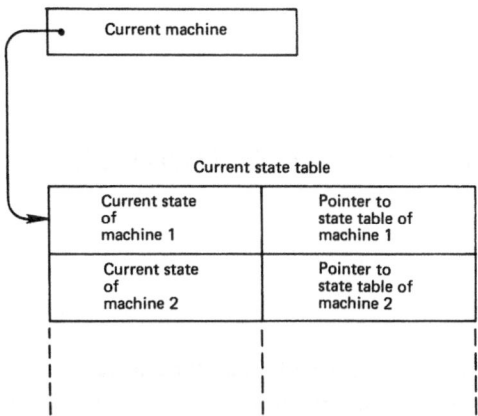

Figure 7.8 Current state table

7.4 SUMMARY

In order to make the design of real-time processes a manageable task, and to minimise the complexity of their implementation, it is necessary to employ a virtual machine abstraction. High-level language compilers provide useful general-purpose virtual machines. Moreover, it is possible, at relatively little cost, to provide software to support special-purpose virtual machines that are tailored to the requirements of a specific set of processes.

The implementation of the two special-purpose virtual machines described in this chapter are examples of the general technique of writing *table-driven* software. The idea is to produce a small, general-purpose program which will define its actions by looking up instructions in data tables. A major advantage of this technique is that the performance of a particular system can be altered by simply altering the contents of the tables.

Concepts

High-level languages; interpreters; finite state machines; state transition diagrams; table-driven code

8 Performance Measurement

During all phases of the production of a real-time system, it is necessary to be able to measure the performance of those parts of the system already constructed, and to predict the behaviour of parts of the system yet to be built. Without these measurements, it is difficult or impossible for the designer to gauge whether the system is going to meet its performance requirements. In order to *predict* the behaviour of part or all of the system, the designer uses *system models*. To gauge the performance characteristics of existing parts of the system, he uses *performance monitors*.

A designer constructs models of aspects of the projected system so that he may gain an insight into how different design decisions will affect the final performance of the system. He either builds a mathematical or *analytical* model or he simulates the performance of the system using a computer-based *simulation* model. By manipulating these models, he can gauge the effects of alterations or extensions to the system design.

At some point during system development, a decision must be made as to what computing hardware will be used in the final system. It is necessary to compare the performance of different hardware systems in the light of the requirements of the system being constructed. To do this it is necessary to model hardware performance as a set of meaningful parameters that can be used to compare competing hardware systems.

Once the system is constructed, it is possible to obtain an accurate measure of system performance. From this it is possible to ensure that the system meets its requirements and to highlight any areas needing further optimisation or testing. Performance-measuring tools, both in hardware and software, are used to derive these measurements.

This chapter will discuss the modelling techniques used to predict system behaviour and the monitoring techniques that can be used to measure the performance of an existing system.

8.1 MODELLING TECHNIQUES

The two modelling techniques, analytical and simulation, apply a simulated workload to a model of the system in order to derive performance parameters.

8.1.1 An Analytical Model — The Queue

The queueing model consists of a system of *servers* interconnected by queues of *customers* or jobs to be done. Figure 8.1 shows four servers interconnected by four queues of customers. In a real-time environment, the customers will normally take the form of interprocess messages which must be processed by the system processes acting as servers. Examples of customers include individual transactions waiting to be processed by the input process of an on-line transaction system, or records waiting to be written to disc. We can also consider processes which share a serially re-useable piece of code to be customers. The processes must queue up to be served by the code element.

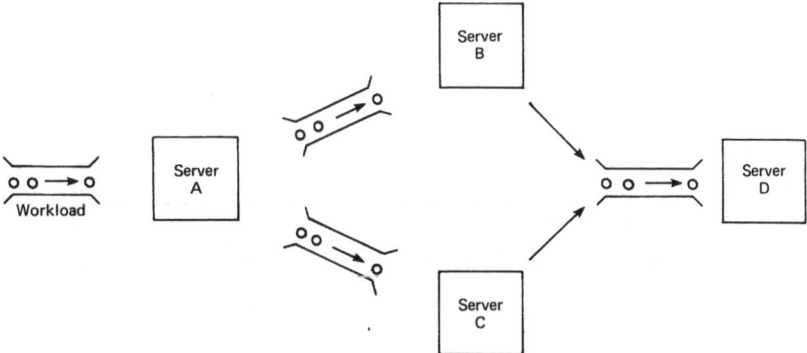

Figure 8.1 Typical analytical–statistical model structure

In order to specify fully an analytical queue model of a system, it is necessary to define the arrival pattern and service distribution of the workload, the capacity of the servers and the scheduling discipline used by the servers.

Customer-arrival pattern   A customer is drawn from a set of possible customers, called a *population* or *input source.* For simple analyses, this population is assumed to be infinite. This assumption makes for a more tractable model, since the number of customers in the queue will not reduce the size of the population. A second simplifying assumption is that the pattern of customer arrival is completely random. It is assumed that the time of arrival of a customer is totally independent of the time of arrival of the previous customer, and that a mean arrival rate can be specified. This pattern is conventionally termed a Poisson arrival pattern.

For a Poisson arrival pattern, the probability that a customer will arrive within a time x after the arrival of the last customer can be expressed as

$$F(x) = 1 - e^{-x\lambda} \tag{8.1}$$

where λ is the average arrival rate of customers and where the function takes the value unity for 100 per cent probability. Figure 8.2 plots this function. Note that the probability of a customer arriving gradually approaches unity as the inter-arrival time is extended. We state that a Poisson process has inter-arrival times that are *exponentially distributed* with a mean of $1/\lambda$.

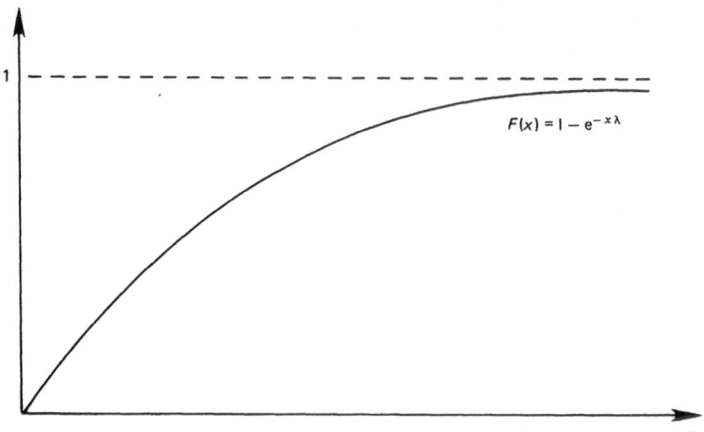

$$F(x) = 1 - e^{-x\lambda}$$

Figure 8.2 Exponential cumulative distribution function

Workload distribution   Once a customer arrives at a server, it will require a certain amount of service. What constitutes this service demand will, of course, depend on the system being modelled. It could consist of a number of CPU instructions to be executed, a number of disc accesses or perhaps an amount of information to be transferred down a communication channel. For most simple analyses, it is assumed that the service demand is the same for all customers and that it can be described as a simple probability distribution of service demands. Most simple solutions use an exponential distribution of service times.

The server   Next, the nature of the server must be modelled. The rate at which it is expected to service customers must be defined. The average service time can readily be derived

$$\text{average expected service time} = \frac{\text{average service demand}}{\text{server's capacity}}$$

or in conventional symbols

$$\bar{x} = \frac{\bar{S}}{C} \tag{8.2}$$

The *capacity*, C, depends on the system being modelled. For example, a server modelling a CPU would have its capacity expressed in units of million instructions per second.

The inverse of the service time, the completion rate, is given the symbol μ.

Scheduling discipline   Usually, the first customer in the queue is the first to be served; a FIFO scheduling discipline. However, others, such as the round-robin and pre-emptive disciplines discussed in chapter 4, are used if applicable to the system being modelled.

8.1.1.1 Measures of Performance

Before proceeding to discuss a specific queueing model, it will be useful to express a number of important relationships. These relationships are regularly used in the description of real-time computer system performance.

First, we can define the *utilisation factor* as the product of the average arrival rate and the average service time per customer

$$\rho = \lambda \bar{x} \tag{8.3}$$

Clearly, this provides us with a figure which expresses the fraction of the system's capacity that is now in use. Obviously, the figure cannot exceed unity. In fact, as we shall see below (equation 8.9), it cannot even approach it.

The system *throughput*, or average number of customers completed per unit time, is another important parameter. The throughput is equal to the arrival rate for as long as this is less than the maximum servicing rate, $\rho\mu$. The maximum throughput is equal to the maximum servicing rate.

Perhaps the most important measure of the performance of a real-time system is its *response time*. For some systems, we can regard the response time as the total time that a customer is in the system. For other systems it could be argued that the response time is the time that a customer must wait before commencing to be serviced. We can state that the average time that a customer is in the system is equal to the average service time plus the average time spent waiting in the queue

$$\bar{T} = \bar{x} + \bar{W} \tag{8.4}$$

Further, we can relate the average number of customers in the system, $\bar{N}$, to the average arrival rate and the average time spent in the system:

$$\bar{N} = \lambda\bar{T} \tag{8.5}$$

This result can be extended to show that the number and time in the queue are related by

$$\bar{N}_q = \lambda\bar{W} \tag{8.6}$$

8.1.1.2 A Simple Queueing System – The M/M/1 Queue

Conventionally, queueing systems are described using the shorthand notation
A/B/m. *A* describes the customer arrival pattern, the inter-arrival time distribution,
B describes the service time distribution; and *m* defines the number of servers
serving the queue. The symbol M represents an exponential distribution, and
thus an M/M/1 queueing system is one with a single server, where the arrival
pattern is a Poisson process and the server times are exponentially distributed.
        The M/M/1 queue is a simple model that is readily amenable to analytical
solution. More complex models may more closely parallel the system being
modelled; however, they require a more complicated mathematical analysis.
Fortunately, the M/M/1 model behaves in a very similar manner to the more
complex models. It can therefore often be used in place of more complex models
to provide solutions that are normally within an acceptable degree of accuracy.
We shall not attempt to analyse the M/M/1 system rigorously, but simply state
some useful results. The first result is as follows

$$\text{average number in the system} = \frac{\text{utilisation factor}}{1 - \text{utilisation factor}}$$

or

$$\bar{N} = \frac{\rho}{1 - \rho} \tag{8.7}$$

Applying equation 8.5 to this equation we get

average time spent waiting in the system

$$= \frac{\text{utilisation factor x average service time}}{1 - \text{utilisation factor}}$$

or

$$\bar{W} = \frac{\rho \bar{x}}{1 - \rho} \tag{8.8}$$

The average total time in the system, $\bar{T}$, is

$$\bar{T} = \frac{\bar{x}}{1 - \rho} \tag{8.9}$$

Depending on how we define response time – either as total time in the system
or as time waiting for service – equations 8.8 and 8.9 relate response time to the
utilisation factor. Note that these quantities are inversely proportional to $(1 - \rho)$.
Thus, as ρ approaches unity, that is, as the utilisation approaches the server's full
capacity, these quantities approach infinity. Figure 8.3 shows the effect. We can
only maintain high utilisation of the server at the expense of greatly increased

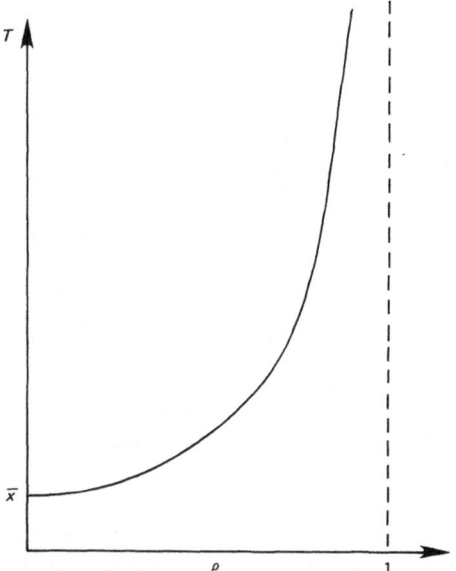

Figure 8.3 Average delay vs ρ for M/M/1 queue

queue lengths. This implies that we cannot maintain a utilisation factor close to one over an extended period. However, in the short term, if the queue length is greater than zero, utilisation must be unity as a customer will currently be being served. Hence, in the long term average queue lengths must either be less than one or else infinity. A queue is purely a technique for handling short peaks in demand.

8.1.1.3 Example

As an example, consider a simple M/M/1 queueing situation (figure 8.4). Assume that the average service time per customer is 1 s and, initially, that one customer arrives every 2 s. Now

$$\text{Average service time} = \bar{x} = 1 \text{ s}$$

$$\text{Average arrival rate} = \lambda = \tfrac{1}{2} = 0.5 \text{ s}^{-1}$$

Therefore, the utilisation factor $\rho = \bar{x}\lambda = 0.5$, that is, the server is 50 per cent utilised.

Furthermore, throughput = arrival rate = 0.5 s^{-1}, and the average total time in the system, the response time is

$$\bar{T} = \frac{\bar{x}}{1 - \rho} = \frac{0.5}{1 - 0.5} = 1 \text{ s}$$

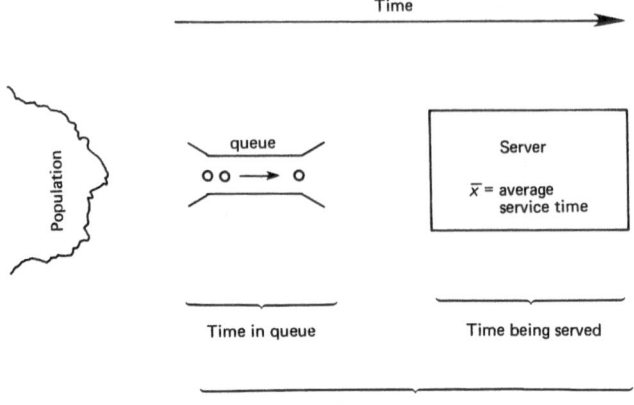

Figure 8.4 Queueing model

Now, as we increase the arrival rate, the utilisation factor and the response time increase. Note in table 8.1 the price, in response time, paid for increasing utilisation of the server.

TABLE 8.1

Average arrival rate (customers/s)	Utilisation factor	Average response time (s)
0.50	0.50	1.00
0.60	0.60	1.25
0.70	0.70	1.67
0.80	0.80	2.50
0.90	0.90	5.00
1.00	1.00	∞

8.1.1.4 Limitations of Queueing Theory

As with any modelling technique, simplifications and assumptions have been made in order to produce results that can be treated mathematically. For example, it is assumed that for a short period it is possible to maintain an infinitely long queue. This is impossible in a real system since the queue must be held in a finite memory. It is for this very reason that a designer is often interested not in the average queue length (the measure provided by queueing theory), but in the maximum queue length, about which queueing theory has little to say.

Furthermore, consider figure 8.1. Whereas for server A we can perhaps assume that the arrival rate follows a Poisson distribution, the arrival rates for servers and C will be distorted by the behaviour of A. Also, if the servers are processes sharing a single processor, their individual capacities will be influenced by the processor scheduling strategy.

8.1.2 Simulation

Unfortunately, the results obtained from the analytical modelling of a particular system may not be open to convenient mathematical solution. Many systems are not readily amenable to this form of modelling. In these situations it becomes necessary to build a *simulation model* of the proposed system. This takes the form of a computer program that models the system under study. While running, the program is closely monitored in order to extract data as to the dynamic behaviour of the system being modelled. Note the distinction between an analytical and a simulation model: an analytical model is a static mathematical approximation, whereas a simulation is a dynamic, operating replica. Setting up and running a useful simulation model is a time-consuming and expensive process. For this reason an analytical approach should be used wherever possible. Simulation is, none the less, an extremely useful technique, and it is worthwhile to take a brief look at the methods used.

The Model

A simulation model consists of *elements* and *events*. The elements model the various items in the system: processes, pools, memory, file areas and the like. In the model, these elements take the form of data structures which contain information as to the nature and behaviour of the system item being represented The data structures are linked together in such a way as to model the inter-relationships between the system items.

The events reflect the changes in the environment of the elements as time goes by. Events include such things as the arrival of jobs to be done, memory allocation demands and interrupts.

Time

The model simulates the events that occur as a result of the passing of time. Two methods are used to simulate time passing: synchronous and asynchronous (event advance) timing. In the first case the simulated time is advanced by a fixed increment. The system state is then updated by determining what events will have occurred in that time increment and manipulating the elements accordingly.

In the simulation of a queueing system, for example, the events occurring during a time increment could be the arrival of a customer on the queue and the completion of a job being serviced. Simulated time is then advanced a further increment and the process repeated for as often as needed to expose the operational behaviour of the model.

The event advance technique does not advance time by fixed increments. Instead, the model is advanced by the amount of time necessary for the next event to occur. The model maintains an event list or 'calendar' which lists the events and the time at which they will occur. The simulation moves through this list, manipulating the system elements as necessary.

The Workload

Two different approaches are taken in providing a simulation model with a workload. Either a statistical approximation of the workload is derived and applied to the model — called a *self-driven* simulation — or actual workload data, derived from a working system, is applied to the model — a *trace-driven* simulation.

In a self-driven simulation, the workload is characterised as a set of probability distribution functions that describe the arrival rate of jobs to be done, and the probable service times required by the jobs. If the arrival rate and service times are assumed to be Poisson processes, then a stream of jobs can be created by applying to the distribution functions random numbers representing probabilities, thus generating an arrival rate and service demand for each job. These simulated jobs are then applied to the simulated 'servers' in the model.

The use of self-driven simulation implies that the designer can derive the necessary probability functions. This may not always be possible because of the nature of the system being modelled. An alternative scheme is to carefully monitor — or trace; see section 8.3.2 — the workload on an existing system or part of a system, building up a set of arrival and service time values corresponding to real jobs in the observed system. This set of values is then applied to the server model. Of course, this method implies that there exists a running system that can be monitored. The technique is clearly of greatest use when attempting to predict the effect of changes to an existing system whose workload can be readily characterised.

Languages

As mentioned above, the construction of a computer simulation model can be a time-consuming activity. However, it is possible to facilitate the production of such programs by the use of special-purpose programming languages. These languages, which include SIMSCRIPT, SIMULA, CSL, and GPSS, provide a convenient way to represent the elements and their interrelationships, handle the internal timing mechanisms, generate random numbers and collect and output performance data.

8.1.3 Simplification

There are some problems inherent in any modelling technique. We accept that the model is a simplification of the real system. However, in order to provide any meaningful results, the model's behaviour must closely parallel that of the real system. The problem arises in balancing this simplification. The model must be manageable, yet not so oversimplified that it loses its usefulness. There must always be a tradeoff between realism and manageability.

Another problem is that of verifying the accuracy of the model. At the early stages of production, when no parts of the system are yet built, the designer will attempt to verify the accuracy of his model by comparing its performance against similar real systems. Once parts of his system are constructed, he is in a position to compare his model against these, and adjust the model if necessary.

8.2 HARDWARE ASSESSMENT MODELS

Hardware performance is usually modelled as a set of parameters; these include clock cycle rates, instruction execution times, store access time, bus speeds and direct memory access speeds. The magnitude of these parameters will have a fundamental effect on the ultimate performance of the system. The problem with this parameter model is that great care must be taken when using any given parameters to compare the efficiency of two different pieces of hardware. The parameters cannot be taken in isolation; they must be viewed in the light of over-all system behaviour.

Take instruction speeds as an example. It is not enough to compare the power of two CPUs purely on the basis of their relative instruction cycle times. Clearly, a fast, powerful instruction rarely used by the system software has little positive effect on the desirability of a particular CPU. CPU performance is a function of cycle time, instruction power *and* the relative execution frequency of the different instructions.

Store access time is another parameter that is meaningless when taken in isolation. A more realistic measure would be the amount of information made available to the processor by a single memory access. This is often referred to as memory bandwidth, and is a function of width of word accessed, bus speed and the existence of cache memories and interleaving. Again, any inference drawn from these parameters must be kept in perspective. Obviously, a fast high-volume link between the CPU and memory will be of minimal use to a system where most data transfers occur between backing store and memory, via a direct memory access channel.

Because of the difficulties in comparing the performance of computer hardware on the basis of parameters alone, a number of other techniques are used to model system hardware, including the following.

8.2.1 Instruction Mixes

These consist of models of programs that are thought to be typical of those expected in the running system. They are mathematical models formed by calculating a figure of merit. This figure is determined by adding together the execution times of each instruction, weighted by the relative frequency with which the particular instruction is expected to appear in the system's software.

8.2.2 Synthetic Programs

Rather than making assumptions as to the expected instruction mix, a program can be written to emulate the behaviour expected of typical programs in the final system. This is called a synthetic program. It is an invented program that does not necessarily perform a meaningful function, but simply exercises the hardware in a way thought to be typical of the future system software. Again, a figure of merit is calculated by summing the instruction execution times. When comparing machines of widely variant instruction set design it is most valuable to base comparison on figures of merit derived from synthetic programs.

8.2.3 Benchmarks

A benchmark is a complete program, written to be representative of a class of programs in the completed system. Usually it will be a program that will eventually form part of the system. The program is actually run on the hardware and the performance measured. For this reason it provides a more realistic workload than is possible using synthetic programs. The use of benchmarks is, of course, limited to existing systems; the hardware must be available and the program written.

As well as being used to compare competing systems, benchmarks are widely used as acceptance tests. In these cases a benchmark will consist of a workload which the system must handle within a pre-defined time span.

8.3   MONITORING TECHNIQUES

Modelling techniques are used during the preliminary stages of system design and development, when the system and its facilities are not yet in operation. However, once the system reaches the construction stage, performance information can be obtained by observing the actual system. This can be done in two ways — by monitoring the hardware or by monitoring the software.

8.3.1 Hardware Monitors

These consist of hardware devices designed to collect performance data. Manufacturers of these devices usually provide an analysis program which summarises the data collected. The hardware comprises a large number of probes which are attached to pins in the circuitry. These probes monitor the logic levels of selected pins at times dictated by events in the system, for example, every hardware clock cycle. The information collected is stored on a magnetic tape which is later processed by the analysis program. Hardware monitors have the great advantage of being totally independent of the system under examination. At a binary logic level, the hardware need have no knowledge of the fact that it is being measured. The resolution of the hardware monitor can be extended to a level below that of an individual clock cycle. It can measure values in any part of the hardware, as well as events occurring simultaneously in different parts of the system.

The major disadvantage inherent in this style of monitor stems from the difficulty of associating the measured electrical data with logical items or events within the software system. Conventionally, the system designer sees the system as a collection of processes, channels, pools, procedures, variables and other logical entities. The hardware monitor can only provide information as to data bus and address bus values, register values, etc. To attempt to translate information derived from a hardware monitor into meaningful behavioural system data can prove a difficult task.

8.3.2 Software Monitors

A software monitor is a program whose job it is to collect and store data concerning the state of the system at pre-determined times. The major advantage of a software monitor is that it can be given a knowledge of the variable names, procedure names, processes and other logical items in the system. It can monitor the system as it is seen by the designer. But software monitors also have inherent disadvantages. Running a software performance monitor can disturb and may even bias the behaviour of the system under observation. This is especially true in a real-time environment where the timing of process activity is so important.

Software monitors are of two types.

8.3.2.1 Free-standing Monitors

Free-standing monitoring processes are activated as a result of certain events in the system. They are usually specified as clock level processes, and are activated when required. Deciding the rate of activation requires a careful balance. The more often the monitor is activated, the finer the detail of performance analysis gained. But the frequency of activation will itself affect the system. The more often it is activated, the greater the perturbation to the system under evaluation.

The monitor process, when activated, stores system status information such as queue lengths and dynamic process priorities in a known location, frequently on backing store. The information can then be processed at leisure by an analysis program, which supplies performance information statistics. The monitor process builds an over-all picture of system behaviour. For this reason, as well as providing the designer with information, it could well be used to supply information to the high-level scheduling process and, possibly, to the recovery system.

Snapshot dumps   As its name suggests, this monitor produces a 'snapshot' of the system or program state at the time it is executed. Typically, register values, variable values, sections of main memory and the status of peripheral devices are dumped to a peripheral (line printer, tape or disc). The information provides a comprehensive picture of the system state at that time. These monitors may be activated on a regular basis, but more usually on the occurrence of a pre-determined event of interest to the designer. They are often activated when the system recognises that a failure is imminent.

8.3.2.2 Embedded Monitors

The second form of monitor is embedded into the measured code by means of a pre-processor or a compiler. These monitors are often included with assertion mechanisms in software development packages. The monitor runs contiguously with the measured code, and is called into action when certain events occur. These events include calls to the executive, function calls or even the execution of branch or jump instructions.

This style of monitor provides a more detailed and accurate picture of the code behaviour being measured but, since it is part of the code itself, certain characteristics may be masked. Embedded monitors fall under two general headings.

Traces   Traces generate a continuous record of events as they occur during program execution. This execution history is particularly helpful at the program debugging stage, when it can be used to highlight the point at which the program commenced incorrect action. Moreover, as mentioned in Section 8.1.2, the output from a trace monitor can be used as input data for simulation models. Unfortunately, this output does not provide an aid for performance evaluation unless it is drastically reduced and summarised.

Profilers   Profilers gather summaries of the events as they occur. These summaries take the form of cumulative tables and provide a useful insight into the over-all behaviour of the program. After the program is run, the profiler produces a source listing of the program, stating the frequency of execution of each statement, displayed beside each statement. This information is particularly valuable because most programs spend a large amount of their time executing a small amount of the total code and the information can be used to highlight these areas for possible later optimisation. Profilers can also help detail the thoroughness of program 'exercise' at the testing stage. After a test run a profiler will pinpoint those statements which have not been executed, and presumably these statements will be the target of further testing.

Profilers provide further information in the form of execution summaries. PET is a typical software measurement system, created for FORTRAN programs, whose assertion mechanisms we discussed in chapter 5. PET produces the following information for a subroutine:

Subroutine name
Number of executable statements that were actually executed
Percentage of total executable statements that were actually executed
Number of subsidiary subroutine calls that were actually executed
Percentage of subroutine calls that were actually executed
Number of decision branches that were actually taken
Percentage of possible branches that were actually taken
Number of times the subroutine was called
Amount of time spent executing the subroutine

Finally, it produces, for the whole program, an indication of the relative time spent executing each subroutine. Experience with the PET system has shown that these relative execution time figures are only marginally distorted by the presence of the profiler.

8.3.3 Properties of Performance Monitors

As the prime requirement, the monitor must be able to extract the necessary performance characteristics from the system it is measuring. This implies that the monitor is in a position to access information associated with the status of the various system entities. It further implies that the sampling rate is sufficiently rapid to recognise every occurrence of all significant events, and that some timing effect is not masking any events.

Secondly, the monitor must cause minimum interference to the system being measured. This criterion tends to clash with the first requirement. The monitor must use the minimum of processing time and take up as small an area of main memory as possible. Clearly a compromise must be made between the above two requirements.

Finally, the monitor must be convenient to use. Unless this is the case, the effort expended in creating it will not be justified. The monitor must be easily incorporated in the system; the user must be able to adjust the fineness of observation and the events which trigger the measurements. Most importantly, the output must be meaningful. The output of traces, profilers and dumps must refer to the logical entities in the system, and not to physical entities such as the octal values stored at particular physical locations.

8.3.4 Levels of Measurement

It is vital that the designer knows exactly what aspect of system performance he is seeking to measure, and what relationship the results of his measurement will have to the over-all system performance. Monitoring tools are capable of supplying a large and cumbersome amount of information. When measuring objects as complex as real-time systems it is often difficult to keep the results in true perspective. In order to maintain his perspective, it is essential for the designer to keep in mind which level in the virtual machine hierarchy is being measured.

Hardware level   Here instruction mixes, synthetic programs and benchmarks are used to measure the performance of the basic hardware under a specific workload. When using these measurements it is important to remember that the amount of parallelism, present in the form of multiprocessing software and direct memory access hardware, may have a greater effect on system performance than raw hardware speed and power.

Executive level   Since the executive level processes are a necessary system overhead, it is desirable to make them as efficient as possible. Suitable measurement will point the way toward areas of possible improvement. The processes themselves can be profiled to highlight much-used code modules. These can then be rewritten with a view to efficiency, possibly in assembler code.

It is also valuable to maintain a free-standing performance monitor within the executive to observe possible inefficiencies in the allocation of process memory, system freespace handling, interrupt handling and so on.

System level   Measurements at this level are directed at improving the over-all efficiency of the system. Again, it is important to be clear on exactly what aspect of efficiency is being measured. A measure of efficiency for an air-defence system could be response time; for a batch-based operating system it could be the maximum useage of resources; and for an on-line transaction system some compromise between response time and processing throughput. Generally, most measurements of performance at this level are directed towards deciding on a correct scheduling algorithm.

8.4 SUMMARY

Without accurate quantitative performance data the designer must make purely subjective projections as to how very complex systems will perform or are performing. This is an activity fraught with risk. Performance measurement provides the designer with firm quantitative information on which to base his decisions. It is applicable at all stages of software development.

At the preliminary design stages, when no actual system exists, analytical and simulation modelling techniques can be used to gauge the effect on system performance of different design possibilities. These models, in conjunction with hardware assessment models, provide an initial guide to hardware selection. Once parts of the system have been built, performance monitors highlight areas of coding and scheduling inefficiencies, and provide an indication as to the thoroughness of testing. Performance monitors can provide data for simulation models, used at this stage to predict the effect on system performance of design changes and extensions and alterations in scheduling strategy.

Concepts

Analytical models; simulation models; workload; queueing theory; synthetic programs; benchmarks; hardware monitors; traces; profilers

9 Current Trends

We have described a number of design techniques and construction tools that will be of general use in the production of real-time software. The ideas discussed are independent of the application environment, size or speed of the system being built. Nevertheless, any design must be brought to the point where it is implemented as software executed by hardware. Therefore, in closing, we briefly examine just a few of the new trends in hardware and software development.

Microprocessors

The multiplicity of real-time systems is being spurred on by the development of microprocessor technology. It is here where the most useful hardware advances are being made. It would be quite foolish to attempt to make definitive statements on current trends in computer hardware. The field is changing with such rapidity that any description of it will necessarily be out of date the moment it is written. However, trends can be perceived; they are all to the software designer's advantage and therefore worthwhile mentioning in this final chapter.

New microprocessor designs are faster and offer more powerful facilities than did earlier designs. Their characteristics have become more like those of large minicomputer systems. The new microprocessors offer a more flexible and powerful instruction set. Their instruction sets are designed for efficient handling of high-level-language constructs. A wide range of addressing modes, efficient stack operators and facilities for writing relocatable code are becoming common-place. These factors will lead the way toward more and more systems being written in high-level language code, offering all the advantages that this implies. Many new microprocessor designs include the ability to address at least one megabyte (2^{20} words) of memory. This, combined with ever-diminishing memory costs, tends to rule out the objection of high memory usage, an argument often raised against the use of high-level languages.

It further implies that channels and pools can be implemented to reside purely in main storage — a significant gain in simplicity.

Most new designs include memory management hardware. This makes it possible to implement the fire wall between user and executive space, and even between individual processes. Additional hardware facilities are being provided

to assist in the construction of distributed systems. These include instructions
for locking and releasing processor access to busses, and interprocessor synchronisation primitives implemented as part of the instruction set. These capabilities
will greatly simplify the implementation of multimicroprocessor systems.

Most of these facilities are not new to mini and mainframe computer
designs. It is very fortunate that they are being included in microprocessor designs
since they encourage the use of structuring and the simplification techniques
mentioned in previous chapters.

PASCAL

Perhaps the most significant trend in real-time software implementation over the
last few years has been the acceptance of high-level languages and, more
importantly, the evolution of a *de facto* standard language in the guise of
PASCAL. Although it is by no means perfect for all applications — it was
originally designed as an academic teaching language — it has gained in favour
because of its elegant simplicity, and has now been adopted by virtually all
microprocessor manufacturers.

Portable Real-time Systems

Research is being conducted on the construction of small efficient, portable
real-time systems. This complements the trend in hardware toward distributed
systems. Wirth (1977) the designer of PASCAL, is at the forefront of this activity
with his MODULA system. He approaches the problem from the direction of
language design.

Conventional real-time languages do not have a concept of 'process' built
into them. Rather they assume the existence of a basic operating system, usually
written in assembler code. Communication with the outside world and synchronisation with other programs written in the language is carried out by calls to the
operating system. The problem with this situation is that most available operating
systems are too large to place on small distributed processing elements. In any
event, most facilities provided by a generalised operating system are not used by
a set of real-time programs.

MODULA, on the other hand, is a high-level language, which incorporates
the ability to specify concurrently running processes and their necessary
synchronisation and intercommunication. The software necessary to implement
the virtual machine (process scheduling and synchronisation) consists of a mere
hundred instructions.

Wirth combines real-time and high level language virtual machines in one
simple system.

Design Tools

Jackson (1979) has developed a design tool combining a high-level language with
a real-time nucleus. The nucleus, MASCOT, provides a real-time virtual machine
very similar to the one described in chapter 2. The CORAL language (Webb,
1978) has been extended to include concepts of processes, channels and pools.
The resultant language, MORAL, (Jackson, 1979) can be used in conjunction
with a sophisticated system building facility to produce real-time systems
running on the MASCOT nucleus. This system is currently enjoying wide use in
the United Kingdom.

A considerable amount of work is being carried out to refine system
specification and design tools. The American 'Structured Analysis and Design
Technique' (SADT) is gaining increasing acceptance, and international bodies
such as the CCITT are developing their own tools.

SADT uses a collection of graphical building blocks to describe both
functions and data. The design is expressed as a hierachical set of diagrams, each
depicting greater and greater detail. The fundamental building block, 'the box',
represents a part of the whole system. Arrows representing input, output, control
and mechanism are used to relate each part to the whole. This technique forces
the designer to express his ideas as a strongly structured set of diagrams.

Construction Tools

Increasingly, software construction, test and maintenance tools are being
integrated to form software development systems centred on a project database.
The UNIX (1978) Programmer's Work Bench is an example. This system provides
a project file structure and a set of integrated software tools. The system runs
with the UNIX operating system on a PDP11 processor, but it is designed for use
in the production of software for any processor.

Today, more and more sophisticated software tools are being made available
to the designer. Developments in software and hardware are easing the designer's
job by facilitating simple, well-structured designs. However, tools are of little
value unless used intelligently. No tool can guarantee good design. The designer
must continually strive to reduce complexity and enforce structure. At all times
his catch phrase should be 'keep it simple'!

References and Selected Bibliography

SOFTWARE DESIGN METHODS AND TECHNIQUES

Bergland, G. D., Structured design methodologies, *Proceedings of the 15th Conference on Design Automation* (I.E.E.E., 1978) pp. 475–93

Constantine, L. L., Myers, G. J., and Stevens, W. P., Structured design, *IBM Syst. J.*, **13** (1974) 115–39

Jackson, M. A., *Principles of Program Design* (Academic Press, New York, 1975)

Kernighan, B. W., and Plauger, P. J., *Software Tools* (McGraw-Hill, New York, 1976)

McCracken, D. D., Revolution in programming, *Datamation*, **19** (1973) 50–2

McGowan, C. L., A review of decomposition and design methodologies structural Design, *Infotech State of the Art Conference* (Infotech, Maidenhead, Berks., 1977)

Myers, G. J., *Reliable Software Through Composite Design* (Petrocelli/Charter, New York, 1975)

Myers, W., The need for software engineering, *Computer*, **11** (1978) 12–24

Parnas, D. L., On the criteria to be used in decomposing systems into modules, *Communs ACM*, **15** (1972) 1053–8

Wirth, N., Program development by stepwise refinement, *Communs ACM*, **14** (1971) 224–7

Yourdon, E., *Techniques for Program Structure and Design* (Prentice-Hall, Englewood Cliffs, N.J., 1975)

OPERATING SYSTEMS PRINCIPLES AND SCHEDULING

Brinch Hansen, P., *Operating System Principles* (Prentice-Hall, Englewood Cliffs, N.J., 1973)

Coffman, E. G., and Kleinrock, L., Computer scheduling methods and their countermeasures, *Proceedings AFIPS Spring Joint Computer Conference*, **32** (1968) 11–21

nan, E. G., Elphick, M., and Shoshani, A., System deadlocks, *Comput. rv.*, **3** (1971) 67–8

Courtois, P. J., Heymans, F., and Parnas, D. L., Concurrent control with "Readers" and "Writers", *Communs ACM*, **14** (1971) 667–8

Dijkstra, E. W., Co-operating sequential processes, in *Programming Languages*, ed. F. Genuys (Academic Press, London, 1968)

Dijkstra, E. W., The structure of the T. H. E. multiprogramming system, *Communs ACM*, **11** (1968) 341–6

Hoare, C. A. R., Monitors: an operating system structuring concept, *Communs ACM*, **17** (1974) 549–57

Holt, R. C., Graham, G. S., Lazowska, E. D., and Scott, M. A., *Structured Concurrent Programming with Operating Systems Applications* (Addison-Wesley, Reading, Mass., 1978)

Lister, A. M., *Fundamentals of Operating Systems*, 2nd ed. (Macmillan, London, 1980)

RELIABILITY AND SOFTWARE ENGINEERING

Belady, L. A., and Lehman, M. M., A model of large program development, *IBM Syst. J.*, **15** (1976) 225–51

Brooks, F. P., *Mythical Man Month* (Addison-Wesley, Reading, Mass., 1975)

Irvine, C. A., and Brackett, J. W., Automated software engineering through structured data management, *IEEE Trans. Software Engng*, SE–3 (1977) 34–40

Ivie, E. L., The programmer's workbench – a machine for software development, *Communs ACM*, **20** (1977) 746–53

Kopetz, H., *Software Reliability* (Macmillan, London, 1979)

Myers, G. J., *Software Reliability – Principles and Practice* (Wiley Interscience, New York, 1976)

Nakajima, H., Dokeh, K., and Tamaki, K., Software techniques for electronic switching system dependability, *Proc. IEE Software Engng Telecommuns Switching Syst.*, **97** (1977) 125–34

Owen, G. J., Rollback – a method for process and system recovery, *Proc. IEE Software Engng Telecommun Switching Syst.* (1973) 118–24

Randell, B., System structure for software fault tolerance, *Current Trends in Programming Methodology*, Vol. 1 (Prentice-Hall, Englewood Cliffs, N. J., 1977) pp. 195–219

Randell, B., Lee, P. A., and Treleaven, M. P. C., Reliable computing systems, in *Springer Lecture Notes in Computer Science No. 60 Advanced Course on Operating Systems* (Springer Verlag, New York, 1978) pp. 282–391

Stuki, L. G., New directions in automated tools for improving software quality, *Current Trends in Programming Methodology*, Vol. 2 (Prentice-Hall, Englewood Cliffs, N. J., 1978) pp. 80–111

QUEUEING THEORY AND SYSTEM MEASUREMENT

Beizer, B., *Micro Analysis of Computer System Performance* (Van Nostrand Reinhold, New York, (1978)

Knuth, D. E., An empirical study of FORTRAN programs, *Software Pract. Experience*, 1 (1971) 105–33

Mansford, E., and Drummond, J. R., *Evaluation and Measurement Techniques for Digital Computer Systems* (Prentice-Hall, Englewood Cliffs, N.J., 1973)

Satterthwaite, E., *Debugging Tools for High Level Languages* (University of Newcastle-upon-Tyne Technical Report, December, 1971)

EXAMPLES OF EXISTING SYSTEMS

Organick, E. I., *The MULTICS System – An Examination of its Structure* (MIT Press, Cambridge, Mass., 1972)

Ornstein S. M., Crowther, W. R., Kraley M. F., Bressler R. D., Michel, A., and Heart, F. E., Pluibus – a reliable multiprocessor, *AFIPS Conference Proceedings*, 44 (1975) 51–9

Smol, G., Hamer, M. P. R., and Hills, M. T., *Telecommunications – A System Approach* (Allen & Unwin, London, 1976)

Takamura, S., Kawashima, H., and Nakajima, H., *Software Design for Electronic Switching Systems* (Peter Perigrinus, London, 1979)

Jackson, K., *The Official Handbook of MASCOT (Draft 1)* (MASCOT Suppliers Association, 1979). Obtainable from R.S.R.E., Malvern, U.K.

Ritchie, D. M., and Thomson, K., The UNIX time-sharing system, *Communs ACM*, 17 (1974) 365–75

LANGUAGES

Ross, D. T., Structured Analysis (SA): a language for communicating ideas, *Trans. IEEE Software Engng*, SE–3 (1977) 16–33

SDL Functional Specification and Description Language in Series Z Recommendations (Z101–Z104) of CCITT Sixth Plenary Assembly, Geneva, October 1976

Webb, J. T., *CORAL 66 Programming* (N.C.C. Publications, Manchester, 1978)

Wilson, I. R., and Addyman, A. M., *A Practical Introduction to PASCAL* (Macmillan, London, 1978)

Wirth, N., MODULA – a language for modular multiprogramming, *Software Pract. Experience*, 7 (1977) 3–35

Glossary

Addressing mode   The manner in which the address forming part of a machine instruction is interpreted as an actual store location.

Analytical Model   A mathematical approximation of an aspect of a system's performance.

Arrival pattern   A statistical description of the arrival times of customers queueing for service.

Assertion   A logical statement describing the expected behaviour of a module at a particular point during the execution of its code.

Audit process   A process designed to check a system for errors or inconsistent behaviour. It compares the current system state with its own inbuilt view of correct operation.

Backing store   High capacity storage not directly accessible by the CPU, for example, discs and drums.

Batch   Mode of computer operation where programs are run in groups. The programs making up each group are selected so as to optimise the use of system resources while each group is run.

Benchmark   A program or set of programs designed to be representative of the expected workload on a system; used to derive information as to system performance.

Bit map   An array of binary digits, each digit representing the state of a system item, for example, on/off, activated/not activated, allocated/not allocated.

Bootstrap   A small program (often resident in non-erasable read-only memory) designed to load a larger program into main memory. This larger program is, in turn, designed to load the remainder of the system software.

Builder (system builder)   A program designed to load the code elements of user processes and to include their process descriptors in the process descriptor pool.

Bus   A set of wires on which data, address and control information can be transmitted from one of a number of sources. This information can then be received by a number of destinations.

Cache memory   A random access storage element of smaller capacity but of faster access time than main storage.

CCITT   International Telegraph and Telephone Consultative Committee.

Channel   A pathway down which information can flow.

Checkpoint   A stage at which a program is known to be operating correctly.

Checksum   A numerical value which is a function of the binary patterns making up a data file or the code element of a process.

Circular buffer   List of memory elements linked or accessed in a circular chain.

Clock (real-time clock)   A hardware device which generates an interrupt at regular intervals.

Code element   That part of a process which consists of executable instructions and data.

Code sharing   Technique whereby two or more processes use the same section of code as part of their code element.

Cohesion   A measure of the strength of the internal structure of a module.

Conditional compilation   Technique whereby a compiler either includes or ignores sections of program code; dependent on parameters provided to the compiler when activated.

Controlled system   Set of devices which interfaces with the environment, whose functioning is controlled by a real-time system.

Controlling system   The software component of a real-time system, together with its necessary processing hardware.

Conversation   A recovery block containing part of the progress of more than one process. All the processes must pass their acceptance tests before any of the processes can exit the recovery block.

CORAL   High-level language developed for real-time applications by the UK Ministry of Defence.

Coupling   Measure of the closeness and complexity of interrelationships between modules.

Data abstraction   Design technique whereby processes and modules are given restricted knowledge of the layout of system data structures.

Data structure design technique (Michael Jackson Technique)   Design technique whereby the form of the data structures in a design define the structure of the code which acts on them.

Deadlock (deadly embrace)   Situation wherein a process (or set of processes) cannot continue operation because another process (or set of processes) holds a resource required by the first process. At the same time the second process is halted because it requires resources held by the first process.

Dispatcher   Hardware or software mechanism which carries out actions necessary to swap a processor from execution of one process to the execution of another.

Error seeding   Method of assessing the success of a testing scheme. Known errors are introduced into a system and the percentage of 'seeded' errors detected is related to the probable percentage of unknown errors that *have* been detected.

Event (significant event)   An occurrence which results in a change in the state of a system.

Event scanner   Process which scans a system and compares the present status of the system with that found by a previous scan and reports the discrepancies as events.

Executive (kernel)   That part of a real-time system which supports the existence of, and controls the activity of, the processes in the system.

Fault tolerant systems   Systems which can continue operation in spite of the occurrence of faults.

FIFO   First in first out.

Finite state machine   A machine or system which exists in one of a finite number of possible states at any point in time.

Freespace   Pool of memory elements (in main storage or backing store) which is available for temporary use by any of the system processes.

Hardware lock/unlock   A method which ensures that process swapping cannot occur while the 'lock' is on. For example, temporary disablement of interrupts in a single processor system.

High-level scheduler   A process which is capable of altering the priority of processes in a system.

Hopper   See Circular Buffer.

Interpreter   Program which reads, interprets and acts on a sequence of coded instructions.

Interrupt handler   Process which is executed immediately on the occurrence of an interrupt. Designed to carry out a small amount of time-critical functions related to the interrupt.

Kernel   Protection domain wherein processes have access to all available machine instructions.

Life cycle costs   The cost of a product as measured over its lifetime.

LIFO   Last in first out.

Main memory, main storage   That part of a computer system's storage which is directly accessible by the CPU.

MASCOT   Modular Approach to Software Construction, Operation and Test.

Memory bandwidth   The amount of information made available to the processor by a single memory access.

Memory management hardware   Hardware mechanism, residing between the CPU and main memory, which maps the address field of a processor instruction on to an actual physical location. Also, usually implements protection domains.

MODULA   A small nucleus of software designed to support asynchronous processes, together with a high-level language suitable for use in this multiprocess environment.

Monitor   A collection of routines which control and protect a particular resource.

MTBF   Mean time between failures.

MTTR   Mean time to repair.

Multiplexing   The sharing of a system resource, for example, the processor or section of storage, by more than one process. The simultaneous transmission of more than one message down a communication channel.

On-line system   System which actions each transaction or event in the controlled system, to ensure that the device and file status is continuously up to date.

PASCAL   Structured high-level language originally developed by Niklaus Wirth in 1968.

Performance monitor   Tool implemented in software or hardware, used to gauge performance characteristics of existing parts of the system.

Poisson arrival pattern   A pattern of customer arrival where the time of arrival of one customer is totally independent of the time of arrival of the previous customer, and a mean arrival rate can be specified.

Polling   Technique of monitoring device status by regular inspection of the values of register(s) associated with the device.

Pool   Collection of data items which are available to more than one process in the system.

Pre-emptive scheduling   Technique whereby the running process may be stopped in order that a higher-priority process may continue.

Priority   A measure of the relative importance of processes in a real-time system. A process's priority may be fixed or may vary with changing environmental conditions.

Process control systems   Real-time systems which control industrial processes, especially chemical and manufacturing.

Process descriptor   Part of a process, consisting of a data structure in which the volatile environment of the process can be stored should the process be temporarily suspended.

Profiler   A software utility which summarises the results of a program trace to provide information on the frequency of execution of different parts of the subject program.

Program counter   CPU register containing the storage address of the next instruction to be executed.

Protection domain   Combination of a process's memory area and its privileges.

Protective redundancy   Technique which guarantees continued performance of the module's functions by including one or more identical, but functionally redundant, modules in the system.

Queue   A list or ordered linked set of memory elements. In queueing theory, a line of customers waiting for service.

Queueing theory   Mathematical discipline concerned with the analytical model of systems that are made up of queues.

Real-time system   A control system which responds virtually instantaneously to change in the environment it is controlling. 'Instantaneous' is a relative measure, dependent on the system being controlled.

Recovery block   A number of alternative code blocks, headed by an acceptance test. All the code blocks perform the same function, but in different ways. If, when executed, one code block fails the acceptance test, then another code block is tried.

Recovery monitor   Process which instigates recovery action when signalled that a fault has occurred.

Re-entrant code   Code segment which can be executed by more than one process at a time without the action of one process affecting the action of the other processes. Also called pure code.

Relocatable code   Code which can be executed successfully irrespective of its position in main storage.

Relocation pointer   Base address of a relocatable code segment. During code segment execution the value of the relocation pointer is added to all address references before they are applied to main storage.

Response time   Time that a system will take to react to a change in, or a stimulus from, its environment.

Rollback   A recovery technique. On detection of an error, the system is returned to a state that existed prior to the fault, and then restarted.

SADT   Structured Analysis and Design Technique.

Scheduling   The allocation of resources (especially the CPU) to a number of competing processes.

SDL   Specification and Design Language (CCITT)

Self-driven simulation   Simulation technique wherein a statistical approximation of the workload is applied to the model. cf. Trace-driven simulation.

Semaphore   Non-negative integer value used as a synchronisation primitive.

Serially re-usable   Provided that no two processes execute the code simultaneously, serially re-usable code may be used by more than one process without causing mutual disruption.

Server   Parts of a queueing system which process customers and therefore process the workload.

Service time   The rate at which a server is expected to service customers.

Shuffler   Process designed to coalesce resident code segments into a contiguous section of main storage, so as to make available contiguous system freespace.

SIGNAL   Synchronisation mechanism. When executed it allows a process to pass a corresponding WAIT operation.

Significant event   See Event.

Simulation model   Software-based model of an aspect of a system's performance.

Snapshot dump   Summary of the state of the system at one instant. Typically the value of the contents of all registers and all or part of the main storage.

Software trap   A machine instruction which, when executed, causes an interrupt.

Stack   A last-in-first-out list of memory elements. Commonly used to hold temporary variables during process execution.

State transition diagram   A graphical representation of a finite state machine, showing the interrelationships between states, events and actions.

Structured walkthrough   A formal meeting between persons concerned with a software module during which the design document, program code and testing scheme are discussed, step by step, in an attempt to highlight inconsistencies and inaccuracies.

Synthetic programs   Programs which emulate the behaviour expected of typical programs in the final system.

System throughput Queueing theory parameter. The average number of customers serviced per unit time.

Table-driven software Programs which define their actions by reading control data from tables rather than following fixed algorithms.

Test data generator A tool which analyses a program and uses this analysis to produce a set of data which when input to the subject program will cause execution of all, or a specific subset of the control paths in the program.

Test harness A set of hardware and/or software mechanisms which provide an environment in which a system, or parts of a system, may be tested and observed.

Test probe A hardware or software mechanism which enables observation of the detailed operation of a system (especially data flow).

Timeslicing Method of sharing the processor by systematically allocating each process in the system fixed amounts of time for use of the processor.

Top-down functional design Design technique wherein a problem is broken down into smaller and smaller parts.

Trace A record or history of events that have occurred during a program's execution.

Trace-driven simulation Simulation technique whereby actual workload data, derived by observation of a working system, are applied to the model. c.f. Self-driven simulation.

Trap See Software trap.

UNIX Operating System Produced by Bell Laboratories for the Digital Equipment Corporation PDP11 processor. Has been transported to other processors.

User space Protection domain wherein processes have limited access to processor instructions and cannot transfer control outside their memory area.

Utilisation factor That fraction of the system's workload now in use. The product of the average arrival rate and the average service time per customer.

Virtual machine A machine comprising software and hardware whose attributes and functions are tailored to a particular area of application.

Volatile environment The information which, if lost, would mean that a process could not continue from the point at which it last executed an instruction.

WAIT Synchronisation mechanism. When executed by a process it causes the process to suspend its operation until a particular event occurs.

Watchdog timer A hardware or software mechanism which generates a signal (or interrupt) if not reset within a fixed timespan.

Workload The service demanded of a system by its environment.

Discussion Topics

(1)   In the interests of simplicity, it has been suggested that a process should be restricted to having only one incoming channel, but as many outgoing channels as it may require. For the same reasons, pools should have one 'writing' input, but as many 'reading' outputs as required. Do these constitute a realistic set of design constraints?

(2)   In section 2.4 we described a simple management information system. One process, IN, was allocated to scan the input locations of all the terminals and another, OUT, allocated to output characters to the terminals. An alternative approach would be to allocate a separate process to each terminal. Would this be a simpler model?

(3)   Take the discussion in topic (2) a step further. In the example in section 2.4, a process was allocated to each activity in the system. Another approach would be to specify that one process carries out all the activities required of one transaction (logging in, reading or writing). There would, at any time, be as many processes as active transactions in the system. Is this a valid approach?

(4)   As they are defined in section 3.8, the pool access routines imply that a writer could wait indefinitely while readers read the pool. Re-design the routines so that no readers start to read the pool if a writer is waiting to write.

(5)   When using a queue mechanism to implement channels there is always the possibility that the system's freespace queue will become exhausted. Clearly, the system must take some corrective action should this eventuality become likely. In many systems it is assumed that a danger level has been reached when the freespace is 50 per cent used. Is this figure too conservative?

(6)   Discuss possible methods of avoiding or correcting the situation where the freespace queue is becoming exhausted. When the freespace goes below a critical level, how should the remaining queue elements be allocated to processes requesting them? By process priority? By allocating an equal number to all processes? By ensuring that each process has at least one element in reserve?

(7)   Examples of finite state machines include call-handling in a telephone exchange and the recognition of character patterns in a telex switch. Name some others.

Index